COUNSELING THEORIES

A Selective Examination for School Counselors

Louis M. Cunningham
Muskingum College

Herman J. Peters
The Ohio State University

CHARLES E. MERRILL PUBLISHING COMPANY
A Bell & Howell Company
Columbus, Ohio

The authors and the publisher gratefully acknowledge the following for permission to use published materials:

From Mary Harrington Hall, "A Conversation with Carl Rogers," *Psychology Today,* *1* (December, 1967), p. 65. Copyright © Communications/Research/Machines, Incorporated.

From Bruce Shertzer and Herman J. Peters, *Guidance: Techniques for Individual Appraisal and Development* (New York: The Macmillan Company, 1965). Copyright ©, 1965, The Macmillan Company.

From Donald H. Blocher, DEVELOPMENTAL COUNSELING, Copyright © 1966, The Ronald Press Company, New York.

From EXISTENCE, edited by Rollo May, Ernest Angel, and Henri F. Ellenberger, Basic Books, Inc., Publishers, New York, 1958.

Published by Charles E. Merrill Publishing Company
A Bell & Howell Company
Columbus, Ohio

International Standard Book Number: 0-675-09066-0

Library of Congress Catalog Card Number: 72-83704

Printed in the United States of America

2 3 4 5 6 7 8—77 76 75 74

Preface

This book is designed to serve as a guide to the salient features of six schools of counseling. Our experience in counseling and guidance centers, as well as interest in counseling in formal centers of learning, gave impetus to this book. There was a temptation to make the book encyclopedic in coverage, but our review of counseling and guidance literature did not seem to warrant this approach. One may question the inclusion or exclusion of certain theories. The rationale for the selection of the theories is given in the early chapters.

We are aware that much of school counseling is information-giving, regardless of theory. Nevertheless the study of counseling necessitates careful examination of counseling approaches to understand the meaning of each in a school setting. Every school counselor will have to decide whether he proceeds from an identifiable theoretical base or takes refuge in some sort of idiosyncratic feeling.

We think that the information included in this text offers a manageable amount of material to be covered in a counseling theory course for those in counselor education. We have attempted to gather material on six theories and put it into a common outline so the individual points of one system may be readily compared to similar points in a contrasting theory. An attempt has also been made to synthesize writings of various theorists with similar views into a cohesive theory. This was particularly necessary in dealing with the developmental and existential points of view as both of these "schools" are made up of a number of views from a wide variety of individual writers. The chapters on theory construction as well as other key points in the text can serve the student as a springboard for careful consideration of 1) particular individual theories, 2) usefulness of theory in school counseling, and 3) additional constructs needed to make a complete theory. A next course can implement theory into tools and techniques for counseling.

It was with respect and admiration that this organization and evaluation was even attempted. Writers of counseling theory and practice have shared their dedication, sensitivity, and clinical skill so as to help push back the darkness. These men have made contributions to society as well as to the smaller world of counseling. The fact that they have fallen short of the ideal theory does not mean they have failed. They are on the way. In the last analysis some combination of hard-headed empiricists and starry-eyed speculators will discover the ideal rubrics for theory, probably in a number of frameworks. Those theoretical offerings that have preceded us deserve our attention and respect, attention when we attempt to examine detail and respect for the theorist's organization and view of what is ultimately an extension of his personality.

We gratefully acknowledge the courtesy of the publishers and theorists who have permitted the inclusion of excerpts from their works. We are also appreciative of the encouragement and thoughtful reviews of our colleagues who have provided much stimulation for our endeavors. As in the preparation of any book we are particularly indebted to the efficient editorial assistance provided by the staff of the publisher.

We also owe a great debt to Arthur Wills for his editing of the preliminary manuscript and to the indispensable people in any work of scholarship, the typists, Donna Littick and Elizabeth Newlon.

Louis M. Cunningham
Herman J. Peters

Contents

As the weaver elaborates his pattern in the warp of life, the drab filament of apathy combines in mysterious ways with the brilliant threads of hope and love. Those who see the cloth gain but an impression of its pattern. It remains only for those who shared in the weaving to fathom the joys and despairs of its meaning.

Louis M. Cunningham

1 Studying Counseling

Some systematic organization of concepts into meaningful and useful paradigms is essential in the area of counseling. Fortunately, such paradigms do exist. They are referred to as theories or systems of counseling or psychotherapy. "Psychologists interested in the counseling process have attempted, therefore, to create theories to explain events which take place in counseling, often borrowing from the more basic experimental areas of psychology as a starting point" (20, p. 1).* It should be noted, of course, that delineation of a system of counseling is not necessarily useful or effective and cannot be if it is artificially imposed.

It appears at present that systems of counseling or psychotherapy are not well understood by most students pursuing a program of counselor education and they are rarely studied during the careers of practicing school counselors. Yet knowledge of counseling theory should be extremely valuable to any present or prospective counselor.

Theory is organized thinking on a particular topic. It serves to interrelate all pertinent variables on the subject to make what is called a system. In particular, a theory may be applied to a set of consistent postulates (statements accepted as true), and the logical consequences will form a coherent system.

There are three main kinds of theory: formal, empirical, and sociovaluational. Formal theory comprises logic and mathematics;

---

*Numbers in parentheses refer to reference lists at the end of each chapter. Interested readers should refer to the bibliography, pp. 152–54, for further sources.

empirical theory includes science and its applications; sociovaluational theory relates to humans and their behavior.

Theory development can be an elegant way of thinking with
closure in a complete system, but counseling theory certainly is
neither elegant nor complete. Perhaps the variability of human
behavior—accented by social pressure and the temper of the times
—negates a complete counseling system, and the theoretical approaches in this book must be considered in this light.

"Standards for the Preparation of Secondary School Counselors" (4) has been one in a series of standards published by the American Personnel and Guidance Association, the Association for
Counselor Education and Supervision, and the American School
Counselor Association. In many ways these policy statements are
but elaborations of Wrenn's seven basic recommendations regarding
counselor education (34, p. 161). All of these standards state explicitly or strongly imply the need for a course in counseling theory.
Arbuckle (2; 3) and others share a concern for the teaching of counseling. Dinkmeyer has said, "Counselor educators should be concerned with presenting varied theoretical approaches to school
counseling" (12, p. 898).

Zaccaria's (35) concern about counseling is well supported by
Aubrey, who states, "For a considerable time professionals engaged
in school counseling have borrowed heavily from psychotherapeutic
models in an attempt to find a theory and techniques viable in a
school content. A number of factors, however, cast doubt on the
applicability of any psychotherapeutic design to this setting" (5, p.
273).

Systems of therapy or counseling do, then, demand some attention. If only neophyte counselors had trouble with the various
schools of therapy, the problem would have been resolved long ago.
But the problem goes deeper, as exemplified by Carl Rogers' disturb-
ing experience with a group of counselors from different psychotherapeutic schools.

> But then came the jolt. The very portions of those interviews
> which seemed obviously moments of real therapy, were ex-
> perienced by other members as nontherapeutic or even anti-
> therapeutic. And the moments which some others regard as
> clearly of a healing nature, I experienced as meaningless or
> ineffectual, or worse. At the time it was a hard blow to assimi-
> late. It meant that our differences ran far deeper than I had
> presumed. I had supposed that we were all talking about the

same experiences, but attaching different words, labels and descriptions to these experiences. This was clearly not true. (26, p. 5)

One might expect beginning counselors to have problems trying to understand theory, but if the "experts" can communicate with only minimal effectiveness, the problem must be acute. Unfortunately for students, the neologistic tendencies of theoreticians only compound the confusion.

Our key counseling words are ambiguous and misleading. There are a number of possible meanings that could be supplied for each. The words do not have identifiable agreed-upon relationship to significant events in real life. (11, p. 460)

Colby states this dilemma another way: "Holders of different paradigms often talk right past one another because in experiencing the same events they actually observe different things" (9, p. 348). He adds, "in the domain of psychotherapy there is no single shared paradigm commanding consensus" (9, p. 347).

Under such conditions, it is not surprising to find, as Rogers has stated, that therapists are not in agreement as to the therapeutic model, aims, or even what constitutes success or failure. Every counselor is free to think his own thoughts, formulate his own views, and develop his own hypothesis (26).

Colby (9), Matarazzo (21), and Segal (30) view psychotherapeutic research to resolve these differences as very slow. Assessing the progress seems like a turtle stopping to catch his breath.

However, not all scholars believe that psychotherapy as a discipline is moving at a turtle's pace. In his review of psychotherapy Seeman (29) views the research as having great promise, and the same view is shared by other authors (27). Zucker has stated that "work in the area of personality change ranges not from the easy to the difficult but rather from the difficult to the impossible" (36, p. 3).

When one examines the known about theory and research and attempts to integrate it with counseling practice, disparities are evident. As currently practiced, psychotherapy has been oversold to the public (28). Clearly, better understanding and more appropriate research are needed.

There is not even agreement on a definition of counseling. Is it the same as psychotherapy? Attempts to distinguish one from the other have not met with general approval. Nearly as many authors maintain that counseling and psychotherapy are the same as maintain that the two are different.

Brammer and Shostrom (8) and Leona Tyler (32) hold that counseling and psychotherapy are different. They maintain that counseling is concerned essentially with psychiatrically normal personalities on a conscious level, while psychotherapy involves abnormal personalities on an unconscious level. English and English see counseling as usually applied to helping normals (13, p. 127) and psychotherapy as a term reserved for practice by "a professionally trained person, i.e., by a clinical psychologist, psychiatrist, or psychiatric social worker" (13, p. 429).

According to Stefflre, counselor educators are determined that a distinction be made between counseling and psychotherapy, and even if no distinction were possible, one would have to be found (31, p. 16). Stefflre uses Hahn's article to support his point.

> I know of few counselors or psychologists who are completely satisfied that clear distinctions [between counseling and psychotherapy] have been made. . . . Perhaps the most complete agreements are: 1—that counseling and psychotherapy cannot be distinguished clearly, 2—that counselors practice what psychotherapists consider psychotherapy, 3—that psychotherapists practice what counselors consider to be counseling, and 4—that despite the above they are different.(17, p. 231) [bracketed material added by Stefflre]

A number of other experts oppose the position that counseling and psychotherapy are separate disciplines. Rogers has treated counseling and psychotherapy as one and the same (25). Another has suggested that if a distinction can be made, it is in quantity, not quality (7, p. 18). Evraiff states that the problem is one of semantics (14, p. 8). In explaining his position that the terms are synonymous, Patterson states:

> The difficulty in, or impossibility of, separating counseling and psychotherapy is apparent when one considers the definitions of each offered by various authors. The definitions of counseling would in most cases be acceptable as definitions of psychotherapy and vice versa. There seems to be agreement that both counseling and psychotherapy are processes involving a special kind of relationship between a person who asks for help with a psychological problem (the client or the patient) and a person who is trained to provide that help (the counselor or the thera-

pist). The nature of the relationship is essentially the same, if not identical, in both counseling and psychotherapy. The process that occurs also does not seem to differ from one to the other. Nor do there seem to be any distinct techniques or group of techniques that separate counseling and psychotherapy (24, p. 1).

Blocher (6, pp. 10–11) generally shares this view. Albert has stated, "If counseling is necessarily a form of psychotherapy, however specialized, present training methods for counselor candidates are seriously inadequate" (1, p. 124). Wolberg says, "Such terms as 'reduction,' 'helping process' and 'guidance' are merely descriptive of what happens in the course of treatment and do not really disguise the therapeutic nature of the process" (33, p. 3).

It is noteworthy that Gilbert's (16) 1952 summary seems as appropriate today as it was then. His survey of the research shows that guidance, counseling, and therapy do not represent separate disciplines but rather somewhat arbitrary points along a continuum. Counselor candidates and practicing school counselors need to examine critically some of the theories.

The field of school counseling is growing at an unprecedently fast rate. There is a danger that many practices will perpetuate themselves simply because no one has had the time to examine their worth, that theories will be accepted without rigorous examination of their assumptions . . . (23, p. 243).

This book attempts to describe various systems of counseling in a concise and understandable manner, thereby serving as a source both for students in counselor education programs and for practicing counselors who strive to implement theory. If the ultimate goal of counseling is to develop optimal effectiveness for the individual in society (6, p. 5), then it must be reasonable to assume that counselors need to understand themselves and the dimensions of their involvement with other human beings.

HOW WE PROCEEDED

A review of selected current theories of counseling and psychotherapy was undertaken and an attempt made to record information in a uniform way so as to facilitate comparisons and contrasts. Evaluation of contemporary research was meant to be illustrative rather than exhaustive.

Theories in this field are numerous and complex, yielding many possible points of comparison but displaying great diversity at the same time. Some systems contain ideas which simply do not lie within the constructs of others. Thus, although part of the problem of comparison is due to semantics, part of it rests in the very fiber of the theory itself.

OBSERVATION

Observation is the key to the study of phenomena. The basic questions are "What does one select for study out of complex phenomena?" and "How are selection and attention reciprocating functions in observation?" Observation involves attending in certain ways, and the attending involves selection.

For this book, an important question was whether there existed sufficient theoretical formulation to be observed. Also, it was necessary to select and attend to theories with consequent implications for school counseling (22, pp. 1–32). Another purpose would probably involve a different emphasis. These are our opinions based on goals and interests of importance to school counselors and school counselor candidates.

DIMENSIONS OF OBSERVER SYSTEMS

Heyns and Lippitt (18) point out the dimensions of observer systems. (1) Exhaustiveness: What categories come within the framework of any particular observation? How much of the total observable behavior is to be classified into an *a priori* defined set of categories? (2) Inference: How much has been inferred in reporting the observed behavior? (3) Discreteness: How many behaviors blend in with or arise out of other behaviors, thereby making their discrete observation less discernible? (4) Size of the unit: How much of behavior is defined as fitting into the selected categories? (5) Range of applicability: To what extent is the observed behavior representative? How much is individual action, and how much is indicative of a general pattern?

In this field, theory development has centered around counseling in clinical or quasi-clinical settings. Only recently has school counseling gained the full attention of publishing companies. It is difficult to implement theory into school practices. Because of all these factors, the selection of theories for study was a difficult problem. It was necessary to determine which theories are most appropriate to school counselors. Research of literature yielded no source of recommended systems for school counselors. A book edited by Stefflre (31) is the only work on counseling theories clearly written for school counselors. Stefflre's volume presents only four theories, and one of these has been severely criticized for its inappropriateness for school counselors (10). However, the critic did recommend the book: "Graduate students in counseling psychology and their teachers will welcome this book as a much-needed resource in counselor education" (10, p. 982).

In order to choose the theories with some degree of consistency, it was decided to survey two key journals subscribed to by school counselors, *Personnel and Guidance Journal* and *School Counselor,* and the two key journals subscribed to by counselor educators and counselor supervisors, *Counselor Education and Supervision* and *Journal of Counseling Psychology.* Thus, we could determine which counseling and/or psychotherapeutic systems are most discussed in the literature. A study conducted by Foreman (15) over an eleven-year period rates the *Personnel and Guidance Journal* and the *Journal of Counseling Psychology* as the most relevant for counseling. *Counselor Education and Supervision* is listed as secondarily important. The *School Counselor* was selected because it is the official publication received by members of the American School Counselor Association.

After the journals were selected, a tally was made of articles referring to the various systems of counseling. Zaccaria (35, pp. 1–11, 41–60) has noted that a number of counseling orientations have been developed, and many conceptual approaches to counseling have been utilized in the school setting. On the whole, however, the most prevalent counseling orientations in schools have continued to be the clinical or directive approach, the client-centered or nondirective approach, and the eclectic approach. The theories chosen for study here are the ones most discussed in these journals. They are client-centered, developmental, existential, behavioral, trait-factor, and rational-emotive counseling.

Once the theories had been chosen, an effective method of examination had to be determined. Any attempt at subjective determination of criteria for objective judgment had many difficulties. If the rubrics were too narrow, some of the theoretical considerations of individual systems would not fit. If, on the other hand, the rubrics were too broad, no sufficient basis for comparison would be possible.

After reading the theories under consideration, it was decided to organize them into a five-part outline. The following outline was used in reporting each of the theoretical positions covered by this book:

I. Introduction
   A. Introductory remarks
   B. Works stating theoretical position

II. Biographical data
   A. Author
   B. Influences

III. Philosophy and concepts
   A. Conception of man
   B. Related theory of personality

IV. Theory of counseling
   A. Process
   B. Techniques
   C. Goals

V. Summary

VI. Selected research evidence
   A. General
   B. In a school setting, if possible

VII. Implications for school counselors

The secondary concern of gathering these data was that of sufficiency. It would have been possible to examine literally hundreds of references on some of the older, more established theories. Therefore, some means had to be established to determine when enough data was collected. In a sense, this point in the data search had to be beyond "threshold" and below repetition. Sufficiency of data was judged by the following guidelines:

1. Enough data were assembled to lead to clear explanation as determined by the authors of this book.
2. More than the principal exponents' views were examined.
3. The contemporary writings of the theory were examined along with the earlier theoretical publications.

The choice of one method of evaluating a theory over another, even though seemingly objective, is still idiosyncratic and possibly could never be completely defended. Perhaps this alone made the project worthwhile for us because of the continuing dialogue necessary for understanding theories. We hope this text also creates a dialogue among those learning and practicing counseling. As Koch wrote in defending his selection of theories and evaluative techniques, "If many significant lines of work have been omitted, the ones included are also significant—and sufficiently varied to suggest a generous range of problems and tasks that systematists face" (19, p. 4).

All efforts within this enormous task have been designed with three purposes in mind:

1. To allow succeeding researchers to use these criteria to arrive at comparative results.
2. To allow readers of this book to compare readily any of the five criteria of one theory with the same criteria in another theory to see similarities or differences that exist between theories.
3. To provide a clearer and more concise summary of various theories to those interested.

References

(1) Albert, Gerald, "If Counseling is Psychotherapy, What Then?" *Personnel and Guidance Journal, 45* (October, 1966), pp. 124–29.

(2) Arbuckle, Dugald S., "The Education of the School Counselor," *Journal of Counseling Psychology, 5* (Spring, 1958), pp. 58–62.

(3) _____ "The Learning of Counseling: Process, Not Product," *Journal of Counseling Psychology, 10* (Summer, 1963), pp. 163–68.

(4) Association for Counselor Education and Supervision, "Standards for the Preparation of Secondary School Counselors—1967," *Personnel and Guidance Journal, 46* (September, 1967), pp. 96–106.

(5) Aubrey, Roger F., "Misapplication of Therapy Models to School Counseling," *Personnel and Guidance Journal, 48* (December, 1969), pp. 273–78.

(6) Blocher, Donald H., *Developmental Counseling* (New York: The Ronald Press Company, 1966).

(7) Bordin, Edward S., *Psychological Counseling,* 2nd. ed. (New York: Appleton-Century-Crofts, 1968).

(8) Brammer, Lawrence M. and Everett L. Shostrom, *Therapeutic Psychology: Fundamentals of Counseling and Psychotherapy* (Englewood Cliffs, N.J.: Prentice-Hall, Inc., 1960).

(9) Colby, Kenneth M., "Psychotherapeutic Processes," *Annual Review of Psychology, 15* (1964), pp. 347–70.

(10) Cooperman, Irene C., "Theories of Counseling," *Personnel and Guidance Journal, 44* (May, 1966) pp. 982–84.

(11) Dilley, Josiah S., "Out-Thinking About Not-Words," *Personnel and Guidance Journal, 44* (January, 1966), pp. 460–63.

(12) Dinkmeyer, Don, "Contributions of Teleoanalytic Theory and Techniques to School Counseling," *Personnel and Guidance Journal, 46* (May, 1968), pp. 898–902.

(13) English, Horace B. and Ava Champney English, *A Comprehensive Dictionary of Psychological and Psychoanalytical Terms* (New York: David McKay, Inc., 1958).

(14) Evraiff, William, *Helping Counselors Grow Professionally* (Englewood Cliffs, N.J.: Prentice-Hall, Inc., 1963).

(15) Foreman, Milton, "Publication Trends in Counseling Journals," *Journal of Counseling Psychology, 13* (Winter, 1966), pp. 481–85.

(16) Gilbert, W. M., "Counseling: Therapy and Diagnosis," *Annual Review of Psychology, 3* (1952), pp. 351–80.

(17) Hahn, Milton, E. "Conceptual Trends in Counseling," *Personnel and Guidance Journal, 31* (January, 1953), pp. 231–35, as quoted in Buford Stefflre (ed.), *Theories of Counseling,* p. 16.

(18) Heyns, Roger W. and Ronald Lippitt, "Systematic Observational Techniques," in Gardner Lindzey (ed.), *Handbook of Social Psychology* (Cambridge, Mass.: Addison-Wesley Publishing Co., Inc., 1954), Vol. I, pp. 374–78.

(19) Koch, Sigmund (ed.), *Psychology: A Study of A Science* (New York: McGraw-Hill Book Company, Inc., 1959), Vol. III.

(20) Lewis, Edwin C., *The Psychology of Counseling* (New York: Holt, Rinehart, and Winston, Inc., 1970).

(21) Matarazzo, Joseph D., "Psychotherapeutic Processes," *Annual Review of Psychology, 19* (1968), pp. 497–508.

(22) Mehrabian, Albert, *An Analysis of Personality Theories* (Englewood Cliffs, N.J.: Prentice-Hall, Inc., 1968).

(23) Nash, Paul, "Some Notes Toward a Philosophy of School Counseling," *Personnel and Guidance Journal, 43* (November, 1964), pp. 243–48.

(24) Patterson, C. H., *Theories of Counseling and Psychotherapy* (New York: Harper & Row, Publishers, 1966).

(25) Rogers, Carl R., *Client-Centered Therapy* (Boston: Houghton-Mifflin Company, 1951).

(26) ———— "Psychotherapy Today or Where Do We Go from Here?" *American Journal of Psychotherapy, 17* (1963), pp. 5–16.

(27) Schmidt, Lyle D. and Harold B. Pepinsky, "Counseling Research in 1963," *Journal of Counseling Psychology, 12* (Winter, 1965), pp. 418–27.

(28) Schofield, William, *Psychotherapy: The Purchase of Friendship* (Englewood Cliffs, N.J.: Spectrum Books, Prentice-Hall, Inc., 1960).

(29) Seeman, Julius, "Psychotherapy," *Annual Review of Psychology, 12* (1961), pp. 157–94.

(30) Segal, Stanley J., "Student Development and Counseling," *Annual Review of Psychology, 19* (1968), pp. 497–503.

(31) Stefflre, Buford (ed.), *Theories of Counseling* (New York: McGraw-Hill Book Company, Inc., 1965).

(32) Tyler, Leona E., *The Work of the Counselor,* 2nd ed. (New York: Appleton-Century-Crofts, 1961).

(33) Wolberg, Lewis R., *The Technique of Psychotherapy,* 2nd. ed. (New York: Grune & Stratton, Inc., 1967), Part I.

(34) Wrenn, C. Gilbert, *The Counselor in a Changing World* (Washington, D.C.: American Personnel and Guidance Association, 1962).

(35) Zaccaria, Joseph, *Approaches of Guidance in Contemporary Education* (Scranton: International Textbook Company, 1969).

(36) Zucker, Herbert, *Problems of Psychotherapy* (New York: Free Press, 1967).

2 Theory

THE NATURE OF THEORY

The purpose of this chapter is to present information concerning theory. It is hoped that the reader will understand counseling and psychotherapy more fully after studying the nature of theory in general.

Theory is but an ordering process (Table 1). The term is frequently—but not necessarily—associated with science. The scientist, physical or behavioral, assumes that there is some order in nature. Were this not the case, no purpose would be achieved in the search for uniformities. Any scientific theory, then, is a proposed general ordering that agrees with observed specifics. "The term 'science' denotes both a certain type of activity and the results of it" (37, p. 497). Science could be, therefore, either method or resultant system. "The scientific search for truth, the research, and the resulting scientific system evidently deal with a certain kind of truth and seek it in a certain manner" (37, p. 497). The goals of science are homogeneous by nature; it is the methods that are heterogeneous. "The aims of science are description, explanation, and prediction" (15, p. 10). Pratt has stated that the subject matter of psychology is the same, in kind, as all other sciences; any differentiation among the sciences is only a matter of convenience (33). Science then is a multifaceted enterprise. Some will emphasize that it is a way of thinking as in the "scientific attitude." For others, science is primarily a way of working: the "scientific method." Still others prefer to emphasize the product of the method: the "body of knowledge." None of these facets can be accepted to the exclusion of the others.

TABLE 1

A General Paradigm for the Guidance Process

Nature of Man	His Values	His Personality Systems

Theory Development helps to determine
(and arrives out of the above)

Goals for developing which determines

Processes and

Techniques

within a *Setting* and *Facilities*
using cognition, affect, and psychomotor behavior
to assist or to participate with a person in his
Valuing and

Developing his personality system
in *Action*
which leads to a re-examination of
Theories of Counseling

Based on Joseph S. Zaccaria, *Approaches to Guidance in Contemporary Education* (Scranton: International Textbook Company, 1969), p. 9.

> The safest procedure is to accept them all and consider science as the total enterprise: men thinking with a certain attitude, using scientific methods to produce facts and theories that are ordered descriptions and explanations of the world (28, p. 3).

Those in the field of psychology, one area of science, must see that psychological theorists ground themselves in theoretical concepts before attempting to systematize the world of human behavior. The methods employed by science are indispensable to psychology. The "scientific method . . . is the most assured technique man has yet devised for controlling the flux of things and establishing stable beliefs" (12, p. 391).

Melvin Marx defines theory as "any more or less formalized conceptualization of the relationship of variables. Any generalized explanatory principle" (27, p. 43). English and English call it "a general principle, supported by considerable data, proposed as an explanation of a group of phenomena" (14, p. 551). They amplify the definition by suggesting that theory is more solidly supported than hypothesis and less firmly supported than law. Nagel defines theory by contrasting it with experimental law as follows: (1) Each descriptive (i.e., nonlogical) constant is not matched with an overt procedure for predicting the term; (2) inductive generalizations based on relations found to hold in observed data are not at its base; and (3) almost without exception it is a system of related statements (30, pp. 83–89). In another work Nagel states the case for psychological theory. "Psychic states of individuals; and the complex wholes of social science are never matters for direct observation, but are patterns of action that can be identified only by means of theory—the natural sciences are analytic while the social sciences are 'compositive' or 'synthetic' " (29, p. 363). The common conception that theory exists in opposition to fact is obviously incorrect. Simply because a theory is not completely verified does not make it diametric to fact. Nagel finds it useful to distinguish three components of theory:

1. An abstract calculus that is the logical skeleton of the explanatory system;
2. A set of rules that in effect assign an empirical content to the abstract calculus by relating it to the concrete materials of observation and experiment;
3. An interpretation or model for the abstract calculus, which supplies some flesh for the skeletal structure in terms of more or less familiar conceptual or visualizable materials (30, p. 90).

As can be noted above, any discussion of theory involves some related philosophical concepts, including law, hypothesis, and system. A scientific law is a "statement of regular, predictable relationship among empirical variables" (27, p. 7)—a proposition "supported by such ample evidence as not to be open to doubt unless much further evidence is obtained" (14, p. 288). Thus, a law is man's best attempt to define reality.

An hypothesis, according to Herbert Searles, is "a tentative and provisional thesis put forward upon the basis of accumulated knowledge for the guidance of further investigation and research" (35, p. 231). Marx's definition is more pointed: "Loosely defined, an hypothesis is any conjecture or surmise that states a relationship among variables" (27, p. 8). The hypothesis is clearly a very useful tool to the systematizer of counseling theories. "There are no scientific restrictions on the source of hypothesis. These may arise from uncontrolled observations—such as clinical insights—or controlled observations—such as scientific experiments" (26, p. 19).

Turning now to the concept of system, we find that Chaplin and Krawiec tend to use the term as synonymous with *theory* (10). English and English define it as "the set of orderly and persisting interrelations between parts of the whole" (14, p. 541). To this definition Ford and Urban would add the facet of classification (17, p. 20). Probably the most germane explanation for purposes of this discussion comes from Marx. He states that a system is "an organization and interpretation of the data and theories of a subject matter with emphasis upon a particular methodology and working assumptions" (27, p. 43).

Psychological theory can be seen as but another facet of science. Counseling theory is distinguished from the general subject matter of science only as a matter of convenience and not because of a difference in kind. Any science has as its base attitude, method, and body of knowledge.

Testability is one of the fundamental properties of theory. A theory probably grows from a hypothesis or conjecture which is also testable. Sometimes more organized theories or collections of theories are called *systems.* The term *system,* however, in many respects, differs little from *theory.* When verification is established for a theory, it is said to be *law;* that is, a predictable relationship between variables has been established.

One could postulate that theories of counseling start as conjectures or hypotheses of therapists. When verification procedures become more acute, these systems often become law.

> Wise men have long known that the business of science is the induction of generalities from observed particulars, and these generalities form the theories and laws which constitute the body of scientific fact (7, p. 9).

In spite of the methodological difficulties in systematizing behaviors of human beings, the scheme of science still provides a pattern by which a framework of knowledge may be constructed. Mill shares this optimism: "But, after all has been said which can be said, it remains incontestable that there exist uniformities of succession among states of mind and that these can be ascertained by observation and experiment" (25, p. 315).

FUNCTION OF THEORY

The function of theory in contemporary psychology is apparent. As Chaplain and Krawiec say,

> Both contemporary psychology and contemporary science in general are an admixture of fact and theory, and since theory

attempts to bridge gaps in factual knowledge, or go beyond what is known, it is necessarily someone's point of view (10, p. 3).

Hall and Lindzey (18, pp. 10–15) describe three functions of theory. They see a theory as a "set of convictions," thus implying that a theory is not predetermined in some way by nature, but is created by the theorist. They stipulate that theory should permit "incorporation of known empirical findings" within some consistent framework. It is a means of organizing all that is known about an event or series of related events. Finally they say that theory serves to "prevent the observer from being dazzled by the full-blown complexity of natural or concrete events." In other words a theory is a limiter, separating the necessary from the superfluous.

In a cogent discussion of theory, Marx says that "several distinct functions are subsumed by theory. Most of these may be summarized by the statement that all theory tends to be both a tool and a goal" (27, p. 5). An investigator uses theory as a tool to generate insights not otherwise possible. The goal function is evident from the utility of theories in the codification and systematic storage of data. Theory tends to focus rather than diffuse attention, and without it little would be possible in the way of systematic investigation or description.

It should be noted, however, that much of what superficially passes for theory in human relations is nothing other than "cracker barrel" speculation.

> Some psychologists substitute, often quite unconsciously, phenomenological introspection and anthropomorphic thinking for theorizing. There is, of course, nothing wrong with such introspection: it has often served as a means of formulating interesting and valuable experiments. In such instances, however, the credit should not be given to theory (36, pp. 66–67).

THE ADEQUACY OF THEORY

A theory is more than good or bad or, as Hall and Lindzey have said, "useful or not useful" (18, p. 11). A theory must meet certain over-all criteria of formal adequacy if it is to be considered generally valuable. Salvatore Maddi (23, p. 451) has listed the following six criteria of judgment:

1. "A theory should be important." Usually theories are not evaluated on a continuum ranging from the trivial to the important.

Evaluation on this basis is difficult because of lack of agreement within the academic community. "The polemic use of terms such as 'inconsequential,' 'limited,' 'far from reality,' and so on when applied to theories of behavior misses the fact that science has no dead-end markers" (24, p. 253).

2. "A theory should be operational." This requires careful definition of the concepts being investigated. Results cannot be meaningful unless there is a clear understanding of precisely what is being measured.

3. "A theory should be parsimonious." Overgeneralization and hypothesizing can be death to any theory. Theories should add details and exceptions after the data warrant, not before the data are available. Marx has stressed the same point.

> Since most of our hypotheses turn out to be wrong, especially in the early phases of investigation, adding more hypothetical parts without sufficient data invites trouble. The principle of parsimony should thus be more widely recognized as a safeguard in the application of science as well as a stimulant in its pursuit (27, p. 21).

4. "A theory should be precise." This requirement is nearly self-evident. A theory must be expressed in explicit language that can be understood by those working with the theory. Obscure, clandestine, and neologistic vocabulary should be avoided.

5. "A theory should be empirically valid"; that is, it should agree with experience and observation. The acid test for empirical validity is prediction. Pratt's warning about psychologists thirty years ago may still apply: "They can be most useful to society by staying in their laboratories and libraries, there to remain until they can come forth with reliable predictions and well-tested applications" (33, p. 179).

6. "A theory should be stimulating." Certainly, excitement generated by a new theory is useful to the scientific community, but this should not be based on novelty alone. It should be the excitement that comes when old questions are answered and new ones are born.

Psychological theorists appear to be free to develop theoretical models of unlimited scope based upon observation of human behavior.

> Psychology may describe the facts of certain types of mental activity and formulate the laws of its behavior, but it is not

especially concerned with the problem of truth or falsity of propositions, or the logical validity of arguments as such (35, p. 14).

THEORY AND
COUNSELING/PSYCHOTHERAPY

Ford and Urban state that "the practice of psychotherapy is an applied field. A therapist's primary purpose is not to
establish principles of behavior, but rather to apply established principles to achieve behavioral change" (16, p. 9). On the other hand,
Hobbs (19) sees the complete counselor as researcher in addition to
diagnostician and therapist. According to this view the counselor's
role becomes extremely difficult since, as Rosalind Cartwright has
noted, research and clinical goals often are in direct conflict (9, p.
400).

In practice, the primary role of the counselor is to help clients
or counselees, not to conduct research and build theory. Yet, if therapists do not attempt to verify some of the theoretical statements and
procedures in use, theories of counseling will cease to exist. And
without some systematic point of view, therapists are likely to be
ineffective and haphazard in working with their clients.

It should be noted, however, that a much wider range of behavior must be woven in the fabric of a counseling theory than just the
behavior exhibited in the counseling situation. Theories of counseling and psychotherapy are like other behaviorally oriented theories.
The subject matter may differ slightly, but the human psychological
base must remain the same. "Those who argue that psychotherapy
represents a special condition, sufficiently different from other behavioral situations (and that) it requires a psychology of its own" (16,
p. 9) are incorrect.

> Since it is the kind of question being raised by a given problem
> which determines the type of method appropriate for the an-
> swering of the question, it follows that there will be as many
> different scientific methods as there are fundamentally different
> kinds of problems (31, p. 19).

The method may vary because the question varies, but the source of
knowledge to answer the question does not vary.

Theories of counseling are essentially theories, in the philosophical sense, based on psychological understanding of a broad spectrum of human behavior. These theories differ only in emphasis, not

in kind, from other psychological theories. It is true that the experimentalist may never come to accept the psychotherapist with his
more philosophically oriented theory. The counselor, on the other
hand, may be dismayed at the use of subhuman experimentation in
the attempt to understand human behavior. No doubt both positions
are necessary if psychological theory is to grow.

The counselor's first concern is the client, and he dare not lose
sight of this concern, no matter what the fascination with research
in counseling. "In the long run, psychological theories of therapy
must come to a point where they will make it possible to select the
therapy which is good for a patient and not the patient who is good
for the therapy" (34, p. 115).

THE COUNSELOR, THEORY,
AND RESEARCH

The assumption that counseling is good cannot be
accepted on faith, just as the theoretical positions of psychotherapy
cannot be accepted without some corroboration. The idea that "every professional school counselor spends part of his time in research
activities" (32, p. 165) is an important one if counseling research is
to improve. Research paradigms vary, but "it appears that 'outcome' remains the *pièce de résistance* for research in counseling" (1,
p. 234).

The need for adequate and appropriate research study is well
accepted by any profession or science, and it should be no different
in the field of counseling. In every case, theory is basic to the whole
scheme of research and practice.

> It is my contention that only through possessing a sound theoret-
> ical background to guide techniques will educators be able to call
> themselves professionals. With a well-formulated frame of refer-
> ence educators will be better equipped to handle old data, and
> better able to make adjustments in their thinking for handling
> new data. Without thorough grounding in theory we are techni-
> cians (13, p. 55).

A philosophical examination of the same point shows remarkable
similarity.

> As a first generalization, then, we may say that, in effect, all
> ethicists and psychotherapists cannot begin to think about

health and ill-health, good and bad living, without some frame
of reference or ideal to guide them, as they go to work ajudging
and analyzing (5, p. 45).

In his work on psychological models, Allport (2) has said that our
theories of growth, learning, and motivation must be revised if we
are to achieve a more realistic image of man. Similarly, it is necessary to revise counseling theories in order to achieve a clearer conception of how to assist and develop man. At times and to some
degree, however, "adherence to a particular point of view can have
real utility. It may focus effort and provide a framework within
which to interpret findings" (17, p. 338). As Klein cautions,

> Unless the clinician has a therapeutic plan, his procedure is apt
> to be an *ad hoc* response to symptoms or a product of impulsive
> improvisation. Planful procedure calls for adequate conceptuali-
> zation of the nature of the problem to be solved (21, p. 732).

Many exciting theories have come into counseling in the last
twenty years. For example, behaviorism and existentialism have
become dynamic forces which need to be reckoned with in our young
profession (8; 6). A counselor with a firm theoretical background is
in a position to examine and profit from these positions. There is
much yet to be done to understand the effectiveness of psychotherapy (4), as well as the adequacy of our methods to study this effectiveness (20; 11). "What appear to be the significant differences in kinds
of counseling are, rather, differences in counselors" (3, p. 219).

Without adequate hypotheses to engender theory, and adequate
theory supported by research, the practicing counselor is little more
than a charlatan abusing his fellow man. With much to be done, few
can afford the luxury of theoretical indifference.

Lister (22) believes that counselor education programs could
minimize theory aversion in counselor candidates by (1) using a
better selection method, (2) providing opportunities for candidate
self-evaluation, (3) researching the integration of theory and practice, (4) emphasizing theory-technique interdependence throughout
the counselor education programs, and (5) assisting the counselor
candidate or counselor on the job to conceptualize his work. Thus,
this book gives a base for the counselor to examine key points in
those theories which seem to us to be applicable in school situations.

References

(1) Allen, Thomas W., "Task Group Report One," in John M. Whiteley (ed.), *Research in Counseling* (Columbus, Ohio: Charles E. Merrill Publishing Company, 1967), pp. 219–37.

(2) Allport, G. W., "Psychological Models for Guidance," *Harvard Educational Review, 32* (Fall, 1962), pp. 378–81.

(3) Arbuckle, Dugald S., "Kinds of Counseling: Meaningful or Meaningless," *Journal of Counseling Psychology, 14* (May, 1967), pp. 219–25.

(4) Berelson, Bernard and Gary A. Steiner, *Human Behavior,* shorter ed. (New York: Harcourt, Brace, & World, 1967).

(5) Bertocci, Peter A. and Richard M. Millard, *Personality and the Good: Psychological and Ethical Perspectives* (New York: David McKay Co., Inc., 1963).

(6) Blocher, Donald H., "Issues in Counseling: Elusive and Illusional," *Personnel and Guidance Journal, 43* (April, 1965), pp. 796–800.

(7) Boring, Edward G., *History, Psychology, and Science: Selected Papers* (New York: John Wiley & Sons, Inc., 1963).

(8) Carkhuff, Robert R., "Counseling Research, Theory and Practice–1965," *Journal of Counseling Psychology, 13* (Winter, 1966), pp. 467–80.

(9) Cartwright, Rosalind Dymond, "Psychotherapeutic Processes," *Annual Review of Psychology, 19* (1968), pp. 387–416.

(10) Chaplin, J. P., and T. S. Krawiec, *Theories and Systems of Psychology* (New York: Holt, Rinehart & Winston, Inc., 1960).

(11) Chmeron, William B., "A Paradigm of Psychologic Theories," *American Journal of Psychotherapy, 15* (April, 1961), pp. 205–11.

(12) Cohen, Morris R. and Ernest Nagel, *An Introduction to Logic and Scientific Method* (New York: Harcourt, Brace & World, 1934).

(13) Cudney, Milton R., "Theory Aversion," *School Counselor, 10* (December, 1962), pp. 55–56.

(14) English, Horace B. and Ava Champney English, *A Comprehensive Dictionary of Psychological and Psychoanalytical Terms* (New York: David McKay Co., Inc., 1958).

(15) Feigl, Herbert, "The Scientific Outlook: Naturalism and Humanism," in Herbert Feigl and May Brodbeck (eds.), *Readings in the Philosophy of Science* (New York: Appleton-Century-Crofts, 1953), pp. 8–18.

(16) Ford, Donald H. and Hugh B. Urban, *Systems of Psychotherapy: A Comparative Study* (New York: John Wiley & Sons, Inc., 1963).

(17) _____ "Psychotherapy," *Annual Review of Psychology, 18* (1967), pp. 333–72.

(18) Hall, Calvin S. and Gardner Lindzey, *Theories of Personality* (New York: John Wiley and Sons, 1957).

(19) Hobbs, Nicholas, "The Complete Counselor," *Personnel and Guidance Journal, 36* (April, 1958), pp. 594–602.

(20) Kiesler, Donald J., "Some Myths of Psychotherapy Research," *Psychological Bulletin, 45* (February, 1966), pp. 110–36.

(21) Klein, O. B., "Abnormal Psychology," in Harry Hilson (ed.), *Theoretical Foundations of Psychology* (Princeton, N.J.: D. Van Nostrand Co., 1951), pp. 698–759.

(22) Lister, James L., "Theory Aversion in Counselor Education," *Counselor Education and Supervision, 6* (Winter, 1967), pp. 91–96.

(23) Maddi, Salvatore R., *Personality Theories: A Comparative Analysis* (Homewood, Ill.: Dorsey Press, 1968).

(24) Mandler, George and William Kessen, *The Language of Psychology* (New York: John Wiley & Sons, Inc., 1959).

(25) Mill, John Stuart, *John Stuart Mill's Philosophy of Scientific Method,* Ernest Nagel (ed.), (New York: Hafner Publishing Co., Inc., 1950).

(26) Marx, Melvin H., "Sources of Confusion in Attitudes toward Clinical Theory," *Journal of General Psychology, 55* (July, 1956), pp. 19–30.

(27) _____ "The General Nature of Theory Construction," in Melvin H. Marx (ed.), *Theories in Contemporary Psychology* (New York: The Macmillan Company, 1963), pp. 4–46.

(28) Marx, Melvin H. and William A. Hillix, *Systems and Theories in Psychology* (New York: McGraw-Hill Book Company, 1963).

(29) Nagel, Ernest, *Logic Without Metaphysics* (Glencoe, Ill.: Free Press, 1956).

(30) _____ *The Structure of Science* (New York: Harcourt, Brace & World, 1961).

(31) Northrop, F. S. C., *The Logic of the Sciences and the Humanities* (New York: The Macmillan Company, 1947).

(32) Peters, Herman J. and James C. Hansen, "The School Counselor as a Researcher," *School Counselor, 11* (March, 1964), pp. 165–70.

(33) Pratt, C. C., *The Logic of Modern Psychology* (New York: The Macmillan Company, 1939).

(34) Rapaport, D., "The Structure of Psychoanalytic Theory: A Systematizing Attempt," *Psychological Issues, 2* (1960), pp. 1–158.

(35) Searles, Herbert L., *Logic and the Scientific Methods,* 2nd ed. (New York: The Ronald Press Company, 1966).

(36) Spence, Kenneth W., "The Nature of Theory Construction in Contemporary Psychology," *Psychological Review, 51* (January, 1944), pp. 47–68.

(37) Wolman, Benjamin B., *Contemporary Theories and Systems in Psychology* (New York: Harper & Row, Publishers, 1960).

(38) Zaccaria, Joseph S., *Approaches to Guidance in Contemporary Education* (Scranton: International Textbook Company, 1969).

3 Client-Centered Therapy

INTRODUCTION

Carl Rogers is the originator and outstanding exponent of nondirective, or in current terminology, client-centered, therapy. This system is the first of American origin to achieve widespread prominence, others having grown from either medical or European antecedents.

Rogers has tremendous empathy for mankind. "This deep concern for the welfare of man is the reason he has confined the major part of his psychological effort to the practice of psychotherapy" (3, p. 424). Through research and development of his theory, Rogers has allowed motion pictures and taped interviews to become available to the psychological community, thus opening the door to evaluation of therapeutic relationships.

The client-centeredness of the Rogerian position is nonauthoritarian. The subject is referred to as a client, hence an equal, and the therapy session is known as an interview. This approach has not always been popular. Between 1946 and 1950 many speakers and writers attacked its nondirective point of view (3). However, in spite of this early reception, Rogers' work has ultimately attracted many followers and generated much in the way of useful research which has had a healthful influence in the general field of psychotherapy (12, p. 95). Today client-centered therapy is very popular, if one can judge from the favorable material written.

The ideas elaborated by Rogers have been given not as statements of fact, but as hypotheses. He has stressed the tentative status of his formulations, the necessity for their revision and improvement, and the desirability of submitting them to empirical and experimental tests (7, p. 397).

Through constant change and revision, Rogers has attempted to develop a more and more cohesive psychological theory of psychotherapy, a theory which has grown out of his experience as a therapist in trying to order those things that seem to be important (25). In a study of Rogerian thought, Dallis establishes the following periods: the eclectic, 1933–1939; the nondirectivist, 1940–1948; the client-centered therapist, 1949–1956; and the existential phenomenologist, 1957– (6). It is interesting to note the fairly parallel periods in the development of client-centered therapy as listed by Hart; he notes nondirective psychotherapy, 1940–1950; reflective psychotherapy, 1950–1957; and experimental psychotherapy, 1957–1970 (13, p. 4). In the last seven or eight years Rogers has focused his attention on encounter groups and principles of education (31). In spite of the shifts, one element has remained constant in all of the client-centered writings: man has the capacity to cope with his concerns when provided with the freedom and safety to do so (6).

Much of what Rogers has discovered in his research comes from personal values and convictions. He has called these convictions "significant learnings." These learnings are (26, pp. 15–27):

1. In my relationship with persons I have found that it does not help, in the long run, to act as though I were something that I am not.
2. I find I am more effective when I can listen acceptantly to myself, and can be myself.
3. I have found it of enormous value when I can permit myself to understand another person.
4. I have found it enriching to open channels whereby others can communicate their feelings, their private perceptual worlds, to me.
5. I have found it highly rewarding when I can accept another person.
6. The more I am open to the realities in me and in the other person, the less do I find myself wishing to rush in to "fix things."
7. I can trust my experience.
8. Evaluation by others is not a guide for me.
9. Experience is, for me, the highest authority.
10. I enjoy the discovering of order in experience.

11. The facts are friendly.
12. What is most personal is most general.
13. It has been my experience that persons have a basically positive direction.
14. Life, at its best, is a flowing, changing process in which nothing is fixed.

Reflections of these attitudes can be seen in all of Rogers' writing. It is difficult to say whether his theory has grown from these convictions, gained from his psychotherapeutic practice, or whether the convictions have grown from the theory. Possibly the theory and the attitudes expressed evolved in unison rather than separately.

The core of the client-centered theory can be found in a number of books or chapters in books written by Rogers. Scores of articles have been published stating parts of the theoretical position, but the major works of Rogers remain the best source of the client-centered framework. His theory can be traced through these works, starting in 1939 when *Clinical Treatment of the Problem Child* was published (21). Other works are *Counseling and Psychotherapy: Newer Concepts in Practice* (22), *Client-Centered Therapy* (24), "A Theory of Therapy, Personality, and Interpersonal Relationships, as Developed in the Client-Centered Framework" (25), *On Becoming a Person* (26), "Nondirective Counseling: Client-Centered Therapy" (31), and *Freedom to Learn* (30).

BIOGRAPHICAL INFORMATION

The fourth of six children, Carl Ransom Rogers began his life in Illinois two years after the turn of the century. His was a large, closely knit family governed by very strict, uncompromising rules in religious and ethical matters. At the age of twelve, Carl moved with his family to a farm where he became deeply interested in scientific agriculture. This was still his primary interest when he entered the University of Wisconsin, but during the first two years of college his interests changed to the ministry. In 1924 he graduated from Wisconsin, married, and entered Union Theological Seminary. However, the dogma of religion proved less than appealing to Rogers, so in 1926 he transferred across the street to Columbia University. Here, under Leta Hollingworth, he was exposed to sensitive, practical clinical work with children and soon decided to shift from work in the philosophy of education to child guidance. While in a master's program, he was granted an internship at a new child guidance clinic whose staff held strongly Freudian views which conflicted greatly with the scientific, coldly objective views prevalent at Columbia.

Columbia awarded the M.A. degree to Rogers in 1928 and the Ph.D. in 1931. At the same time, in 1928 Rogers was employed as a psychologist at the Child Study Department of the Society for the Prevention of Cruelty to Children in Rochester, New York. In 1931 he became director of the clinic, the financial press of his growing family dictating such a move, even though his graduate work was incomplete. It was at the clinic that Rogers began to examine his ideas concerning counseling.

In 1940, Rogers left the clinic to become a professor of clinical psychology at Ohio State University where he remained until 1945. It was during these years at Ohio State that much of his current thought originated. The contact with critical and stimulating graduate students forced Rogers to bring his concepts into sharper focus.

In 1945 he became professor of psychology and Executive Secretary of the counseling center at the University of Chicago. In 1957 he returned to the University of Wisconsin to become professor of psychology and psychiatry. In 1962 he became a fellow at the Center of Advanced Study in the Behavioral Sciences at Stanford, leaving in 1963 to accept a position as a resident fellow at the Western Behavioral Sciences Institute at La Jolla, California. In the early 1970s he was working on insights into the human being as a person and his better functioning through groups.

PHILOSOPHY AND CONCEPTS

Rogers still holds to some concepts (31) in counseling practice which he expressed some years ago (22). These are the beliefs that the individual and not the problem should be the focus of counseling; that more emphasis should be given the emotional, feeling aspects of the situation rather than the intellectual; that more emphasis must be placed on the immediate situation in an interview than on the past; and finally that the therapeutic interview itself is a growth experience.

An understanding of Rogers' special vocabulary is important in assessing his theory, particularly an understanding of the definitions of constructs. Forty crucial ones are summarized below (25, pp. 195–211).

1. "Accurate symbolization." Ability to correctly distinguish symbols.
2. "Actualizing tendency." Inherent tendency of an organism to develop its capacities to maintain or enhance the organism.
3. "Anxiety." A state of uneasiness whose cause is unknown.
4. "Availability to awareness." When experience can be symbolized without distortion.
5. "Awareness, symbolization, consciousness." These terms are synonymous and mean the detection of a stimulus.
6. "Conditions of worth." When the positive regard of a significant other is conditional.
7. "Congruence, congruence of self and experience." The integration of the concept of self and experience.
8. "Contact." When two people sense each other they are in contact.
9. "Defense, defensiveness." Perceptual distortion of experience in awareness to maintain current self structure.
10. "Distortion in awareness, denial to awareness." The blocking of the admission to awareness of material which is inconsistent.
11. "Empathy." The perception of the internal frame of reference of another with emotional components but always in an "as if" condition.
12. "Experience" (noun). All that is going on within the organism at any moment which is potentially available to awareness.
13. "Experience" (verb). To receive within the organism the impact of sensory and/or psychological events.
14. "Extensionality." The seeing of experience in limited, differentiated terms; awareness of different levels of abstraction.
15. "External frame of reference." To perceive only from one's own internal frame of reference.
16. "Feeling, experiencing a feeling." Emotionally tinged experience together with its personal meaning.
17. "Ideal self." The self-concept an individual would like to possess.

18. "Incongruence between self and experience." A dissimilarity between what a person perceives and his actual experience with himself.
19. "Intensionality." The characteristic of behavior of the individual who is in a defensive state.
20. "Internal frame of reference." All of the realm of experience which is available to awareness.
21. "Locus of evaluation." The source of evidence as to values.
22. "Mature, maturity." To perceive realistically in an extensional manner.
23. "Need for positive regard." A learned need commonly developed in early infancy, love.
24. "Need for self-regard." A learned need related to the satisfaction of the need for positive regard by others.
25. "Openness to experience." When an individual is in no way threatened.
26. "Organismic valuing process." An on-going process in which values are never fixed or rigid.
27. "Perceive, perception." A hypothesis for action which comes into awareness.
28. "Positive regard." When the perception of some self-experience in another makes a positive difference in one's experiential field.
29. "Positive self-regard." A positive regard satisfaction associated with the self. The individual is his own significant other.
30. "Psychological adjustment." All experiences may be assimilated on a symbolic level into the self-structure.
31. "Psychological maladjustment." When the organism denies or distorts significant experiences which create an incongruence between self and experience.
32. "Regard complex." All self-experiences together with their interrelationships.
33. "Self, concept of self, self-structure." Perceptions characteristic of "I" or "me."
34. "Self-experience." Any event discriminated by the individual which is also discriminated as "self," "me" or "I."
35. "Subceive, subception." An ability to discriminate an experience without symbolization in awareness.
36. "Tendency toward self-actualization." The actualization of that portion of the experience of the organism which is symbolized in the self.

37. "Threat." A state which exists when an experience is perceived or subceived as incongruent with the structure of the self.
38. "Unconditional positive regard." To "prize" another.
39. "Unconditional self-regard." An individual's perception that no self-experience can be discriminated as more or less worthy of positive regard than any other.
40. "Vulnerability." A state of incongruence between the self and experience.

CONCEPTION OF MAN

The nature of man as postulated under the client-centered framework is somewhat different from that commonly conceived by psychologists. Man is seen as basically rational, self-actualizing, and realistic (26). He has the capacity to experience his psychological maladjustment, organize his self-concept, and experience regard and empathy for others (31). These views of man may evolve from Rogers' experience in therapy rather than the therapy evolving from the concepts. Coulson's study of client-centered philosophy states that Rogers has a Rousseauist view of human nature and feels that the core of man's nature is positive (5). Psychotherapy then becomes the releasing of an already existing capacity in a potentially competent person (31). Patterson sees Rogers' views as being existential and close to Allport's idea of becoming (19). Philosophically Rogers admits he is an optimistic existentialist (11, p. 62).

RELATED THEORY OF PERSONALITY

Carl Rogers made an early attempt to delineate a theory of personality in 1947 (23). Only loosely organized, this effort was based, like his theory of therapy, upon experience as a counselor. Of his personality theory, Rogers has said: "It may be well to note that the initial propositions of this theory are those furthest from the matrix of our experience and hence are most suspect" (25).

Rogers feels that his theory of personality has been completely stated in his chapter in Koch's *Psychology: A Study of a Science* (25). It seems to represent a synthesis of phenomenology as presented by Syngg and Combs; holistic and organismic theory as developed in the writings of Goldstein, Maslow, and Angyal; and Sullivan's interpersonal theory (10). Other writers evaluate Rogers' theory as primarily organismic (15), phenomenological (16), or self-theoretic (3). One recent major personality text fails to mention Rogers' theory at all (14).

Rogers' personality theory contains ten elements which are summarized as follows (31):

1. "Characteristics of the Human Infant." An infant perceives his experience as reality and has a predisposition toward actualizing his organism in the reality thus perceived. He behaves as an organized whole. He engages in an organismic valuing process using his actualizing tendency to value experience. His behavior moves toward positively valued experiences and away from those negatively valued.

2. "Development of the Self." Part of the actualizing tendency becomes differentiated and symbolized in awareness, which is described as self-experience. The representation of awareness becomes elaborated, through interaction with the environment, into a concept of self.

3. "Need for Positive Regard." The need for positive regard, universal in human beings, develops from the awareness of self. The satisfaction of this need is based on inferences regarding the experimental field of another. It is reciprocal in that when an individual sees himself as satisfying another's positive-regard need, he experiences satisfaction of his own need for positive regard. It is, therefore, associated with a very wide range of individual experiences. The need for positive regard of any social other is communicated to the total-regard complex which the individual associates with another; consequently, the expression of positive regard by a significant other can become more compelling than the organismic valuing process.

4. "Development of the Need for Self-Regard." Positive-regard transactions associated with particular self-experience independent of the transactions of social others is called self-regard. The need for self-regard is a learned need developing out of self-experience and the need for positive regard. The individual thus experiences positive regard independently of social others. All of these are communicated to the total self-regard complex.

5. "Development of Conditions of Worth." Self-regard increases in selectivity as significant others distinguish the self-experiences of the individual as worthy of positive regard. If the individual should experience only unconditional positive regard, no conditions of worth would develop. Self-regard would be unconditional, hence at no variance with

organismic evaluation. The person would be hypothetically fully functioning.

6. "Development of Incongruence between Self and Experience." The need for self-regard causes the individual to perceive his experience selectively in terms of the conditions of worth. Experiences in accord with his conditions of worth are accurately symbolized in awareness. Those not in accord are denied awareness. Consequently, some experiences now occur which are not recognized as self-experience, and incongruence between self and experience, psychological maladjustment, and vulnerability exist to some degree.

7. "Development of Discrepancies in Behavior." Incongruence between self and experience leads to incongruence in behavior. Some behaviors maintain the self-concept by being consistent with it. Other behaviors are distorted in a selective fashion, or unrecognized, in such a way as to be consistent with the self.

8. "Experience of Threat and the Process of Defense." When an organism continues to experience an event which is incongruent with the self-structure, this is subceived as threatening. The nature of threat is that if the experience were accurately symbolized in awareness, the self-concept would no longer be consistent; hence, the conditions of worth would be violated and the need for self-regard frustrated. Anxiety would exist. The process of defense prevents these events from occurring by selective perception or distortion of experience. Rigidity, distortion, and inaccurate perception of reality result due to omission of data and intensionality.

9. "Process of Breakdown and Disorganization." When an individual has a large degree of incongruence between self and experience that occurred suddenly or with a high degree of obviousness, then his organismic defense cannot operate successfully. As a result, incongruence is subceived and anxiety experienced. The process of defense being unsuccessful, a state of disorganization results. The organism at times behaves in ways consistent with the experiences which have been distorted and at times consistent with the concept of self with its distorted experiences.

10. "Process of Reintegration." In order for the process of defense to be reversed, there must be a decrease in the conditions of worth and an increase in unconditional self-regard.

The communicated unconditional positive regard of a significant other is a way of achieving these conditions. In order for unconditional positive regard to be communicated, it must exist in a context of empathic understanding. When an individual perceives unconditional positive regard, conditions of worth are weakened, and his unconditional positive self-regard increases.

THEORY OF THERAPY

Rogers' theory of therapy is based on an independent variable (conditions of therapy), dependent/independent variable (process of therapy), and a dependent variable (outcome in personality and behavior). This type of theory is sometimes called if-then: if this, then that. If the conditions are met, then the process can take place. If the process takes place, the outcomes will follow.

PROCESS

Rogers' complete theory of therapy is found in two sources. The following discussion is only slightly modified from these (25, pp. 212–20; 31, pp. 170–76). For therapy to occur the following conditions must be met:

1. Two people are in contact.
2. One of the people (client) is in a state of incongruence, being vulnerable or anxious.
3. One of the people (therapist) is congruent in the relationship.
4. The therapist experiences unconditional positive regard with the client.
5. The therapist experiences empathic understanding of the client's internal frame of reference.
6. At least to a small degree the client perceives conditions 4 and 5.

If these conditions are met, a process with the following characteristics may occur:

1. The client becomes free to express his feelings through verbal and motor channels.
2. The client's expressed feelings increasingly have reference to the self, rather than the nonself.

3. The client increasingly differentiates and discriminates the objects of his feelings and perceptions. His experiences are better symbolized.
4. The client's expressed feelings increasingly have reference to the incongruity between certain of his experiences and his concept of self.
5. The client comes to experience in awareness the threat of such incongruence.
6. The client expresses fully, in awareness, feelings which have in the past been denied to or distorted in awareness.
7. The client's self-concept becomes reorganized to assimilate and include these experiences which have been previously distorted or denied in awareness.
8. As the client's reorganization of the self-structure continues, his concept of self becomes increasingly congruent with his experiences.
9. The client is increasingly able to experience the therapist's unconditional positive regard.
10. The client increasingly feels unconditional positive self-regard.
11. The client begins to experience himself as the focus of evaluation.
12. The client begins to experience less in terms of his conditions of worth and more in terms of organismic valuing process.

TECHNIQUES

Rogers has stated that his emphasis "has shifted from counselor technique attitude and philosophy, with a new recognition of the importance of technique from a more sophisticated level" (24, p. 14). Techniques should be ways to facilitate philosophy and attitudes; that is, they should grow out of the relationship rather than the relationship growing from them.

Thus, the relationship between counselor and client now becomes the crux of the technique. The counselor should bring to the relationship the following characteristics (18, p. 421):

1. "Acceptance." The counselor accepts the client without evaluation or judgment, either positive or negative. The client is prized and accepted unconditionally.
2. "Congruence." The counselor is congruent in that there is no contradiction between what he does and what he says.

3. "Understanding." The counselor is able to see the client in an accurate empathic way. He possesses connotative as well as cognitive understanding.
4. "Communicating These Characteristics." The counselor must be able to communicate acceptance, congruence, and understanding to the client in such a way as to make the counselor's feelings clear to the client.
5. "The Resulting Relationship." A supportive relationship secure and free from threat will occur from the above techniques.

GOALS

The process of therapy leads to these outcomes in personality and behavior (25, pp. 212–20; 31, pp. 170–76):

1. The client is less defensive and more congruent and open to his experience.
2. The client is more realistic, objective, and extensional in his perceptions.
3. He is more effective at problem solving.
4. His psychological adjustment is closer to optimum.
5. His vulnerability to threat is reduced because of the increased congruence of self and experience.
6. As a consequence of outcome 2, his perception of his ideal self is more achievable and more realistic.
7. The self becomes more congruent with the ideal self as a result of outcomes 4 and 5.
8. As a result of 4 and 7 all tension is reduced.
9. The client has an increased degree of positive self-regard.
10. The client perceives the locus of evaluation and the locus of choice within himself. He feels more confident and self-directing. His values now are determined by his organismic valuing process.
11. The client perceives others more realistically and accurately as a result of outcomes 1 and 2.
12. The client experiences more acceptance of others.
13. The client accepts more behaviors as belonging to the self, and, conversely, behaviors disowned as self-experience are decreased.
14. The client's behavior is evaluated by others as more socialized and mature.

15. As a consequence of outcomes 1, 2, and 3, behavior is more creative, adaptive, and fully expressive of his own purposes and values.

SUMMARY

An underlying assumption of client-centered counseling is that man is rational, constructive, and forward moving (6; 26, pp. 90–92, 194–95). He has within him the capacity for positive development. The theory is based on a phenomenological conception of human behavior; i.e., each person has a phenomenal field which determines his behavior. Values which become part of the individual's phenomenal field may be derived from direct experience or taken from others. Therefore, the therapist places emphasis on the counseling relationship rather than some past event. "Instead of focusing on the diagnostic or causative elements of behavior," Rogers has "always been more concerned with the dynamics of interaction" (11, p. 65). Constructive personality change is based upon the therapist's attitudes as well as those of the client (28; 27).

Client-centered therapy is a process where reorganization of the self takes place so the client can more accurately symbolize his feelings, reduce vulnerability to threat, and attain a more positive self-regard. Says Rogers, "If I have made a contribution it is around the central theme that the potential of the individual can be released providing the proper psychological climate is created" (11, p. 65).

Rogers' theoretical contributions have grown from his client-therapist interactions. His theory of therapy preceded the development of his theory of personality. Later theoretical applications have grown out of a necessity to order and apply that knowledge which has been gained in the psychotherapeutic relationship (25, p. 188). In addition to his theory of therapy, Rogers has constructed a theory of the fully functioning person, a theory of interpersonal relationships, and a theory of personality. He has also attempted to apply these ideas to education (30).

As we have seen, Rogers and many of his followers have offered their ideas as tentative and open to revision. The theory is constantly changing and developing, the modifications serving to clarify or add detail to the original point of view (18, p. 437). The theory is one of the most detailed, integrated, and consistent theories of therapy in existence and is supported by a greater amount of research than any other approach to psychotherapy (18). Studies have been done with psychotics as well as normals (29; 8). Snyder summed up the theory when he said:

> The major factor which differentiates the nondirective method from others is that it is client-centered. By this expression we mean that the direction of the therapy process is essentially in the hands of the client rather than in those of the counselor. (34, p. 2)

SELECTED RESEARCH

Gilliland reports significant gains by Negro adolescents in several educational and personal factors through the use of small groups whose leaders employed an essentially client-centered approach, stressing empathy, positive regard, and congruency (9). Similarly, the group was most capable and effective when these conditions prevailed with all members, and the author implied that these typically "client-centered" tenets were sought. The subjects, ages fourteen to nineteen, were randomly chosen and assigned to two experimental groups, one male and one female, and two similarly divided control groups. The controls received no treatment. The experimental groups met one hour per week for the entire school year. Achievement gains were significant at the 0.01 level in vocabulary, reading, and English usage on the CEAT (Cooperative English Aptitude Test); gains also were significant on the OAS (Opinion Attitude Survey) and the Vocational Development Inventory. Grade point average approached significance. A decline observed in the Index of Adjustment and Values seemed to parallel previous research which indicated personality changes, particularly in aspiration and self-concept, among Negroes in desegregated schools. Other findings of the study showed Negro girls reaching optimum involvement in eighteen sessions, while the boys needed thirty or more sessions. Groups were formed that met throughout the summer and continued into the succeeding school year. Multiracial groups were begun in the latter part of the summer at the initiation of Negro girls. These fruitful offshoots of the counseling program were given credit for improved relations both within the school and in the community.

In an analysis of a tape of a successful counseling case completed by Rogers, Truax investigated the interrelations between nine patient behaviors and three therapist conditions with the idea that differential patient behavior might result from given therapist qualities (35). The nine patient behaviors were: similarity in style of expression to that of the therapist, insight, learning of discriminations, ambiguity, problem orientation, catharsis, blocking, anxiety, and negative-feeling expression; the three therapist conditions were: empathic understanding, acceptance of unconditional positive regard, and directiveness. Analysis between levels of therapist reinforcement and the levels of behavior indicated that the therapist did respond selectively to patient behaviors of discriminations about self and feelings, lack of ambiguity, expressions of insight, verbal expressions similar to those of the therapist, and problem orientation. Additional evidence indicated that four of these five classes of patient behavior increased over therapy time, indicating consequential results from the selective reinforcement process. Truax concluded that therapist responses do appear to result in part from client response, and that therapist responses serve as selective reinforcement of patient behaviors.

Pine has described the results of a study measuring the effectiveness of a client-centered counseling program in a junior high school (20). The objectives of the counseling program were as follows:

1. To motivate pupils to seek counseling of their own volition
2. To help pupils resolve or cope with their concerns
3. To enable pupils to become more effective learners
4. To enable pupils to change
5. To enable pupils to develop self-awareness and "situational insight"
6. To enable pupils to ventilate their feelings, to "blow off steam"
7. To help pupils in their vocational and educational planning
8. To provide a service characterized by those counselor qualities which have been identified as common and desirable elements in professional counseling.

Three sources were employed to obtain data to test the criteria:
1. Tape recordings—Qualitative data were gathered as excerpts from counseling sessions which were recorded to measure client growth and behavioral change and to evaluate counseling skills. All recordings were made with the consent of the counselees, who were informed that the tapes would be used to measure counseling skills and help clients. (Data obtained through tape recordings are not included in the article because of the limitations of space.)

2. Program statistics—In order to keep track of the counseling program's trends statistically, the counselors kept tally sheets and detailed statistics to let them know quickly and easily the types of problems which pupils were bringing (educational, vocational, or personal) and whether the pupils were coming on their own (request) or counseling was initiated from other sources (referral and routine). Additional statistics included the number of individual and group counseling sessions, the number of consultations with parents and teachers, and the number of different pupils using the counseling service.

3. Client evaluations—Pupils were asked to evaluate the effectiveness of the counseling program on a twenty-item questionnaire distributed randomly to a sample of 192 of the total number of eighth grade pupils who had been exposed to the counseling service for two years. Included in the sample were thirty pupils who had not voluntarily used counseling in the two-year period.

The results of the evaluation indicate that counseling was effective in helping a number of pupils in a number of ways. Both the quantitative and qualitative data were generally positive. However, this does not mean that there was no failure.

Another study examined "the effects of client-centered group counseling using play media on the intelligence, achievement, and psycholinguistic abilities of underachieving primary school children" (17). The sample was made up of thirty-three first graders, fifty-one second graders, and forty-two third graders from an elementary school in Toledo, Ohio, in which approximately 90 percent of the children were black. The 126 children in the sample completed the California Short Form Test of Mental Maturity and the appropriate forms of the California Achievement Test. Twenty-four children qualified as underachievers. These twenty-four were then individually administered the Illinois Test of Psycholinguistic Abilities.

It was found that if underachieving primary school children interact with other children and a counselor over a period of time, using play media in a client-centered group counseling situation that provides mutually interesting experiences, and if the children's behavior is rewarded appropriately by the counselor and other children, not only will these children significantly increase their nonlanguage functioning, but they will also significantly increase various aspects of their meaningful language usage.

Salomone reported a pilot study at the Montreal Jewish Vocational Service to evaluate the use of the client-centered approach in job placement (33). He suggests advantages for rehabilitation counselors in using the client-centered placement approach, e.g., helping another person become independent by teaching the client useful ways to explain his skills to an employer and saving the counselor time by having the client take more initiative in the placement process.

IMPLICATIONS FOR SCHOOL COUNSELORS

Social sanction—The approval of counseling in the schools has been reluctant, with the positive thrust coming from a defense act (National Defense Education Act, 1958). Counseling in the elementary schools was still not supported financially until 1964. Now, proponents of block aid to education fear that it will lessen aid to counseling and guidance and want to keep categorical aid specifically earmarked for counseling and other pupil services.

To be sure, there are many counselors in the schools (although many more are needed), but there is wide disagreement over their roles and functions. It would be safe to say that most school patrons see the counselor as a teller or director, someone to help their children learn, get better grades, "study harder." They do not consider him an agent of great humanistic change. Thus, there is sanction, but it is limited (2). Client-centered counseling as a general practice would probably not be approved by many communities, although parents might like the attention given to their children in the process.

School press—Administrative pressures of scheduling and student schedule pressures for getting into the next level of education seem to preclude any long-term counseling which protocols of the client-centered approach indicate.

Counselor fit—There is real question whether most counselors ever shun their deep and long teacher orientation. Thus, they feel uncomfortable in a qualitative, affective way. A more comfortable fit is a cognitive, quantitative approach to "add up" numbers of students assisted.

Counselor-pupil ratio—This is becoming so deeply ingrained as to preclude any change. The ratio of one to thirty-three precludes a client-centered approach, if one is even to intend to move toward that impossible one to one ratio.

Counselor—One of the chief functions of the counselor in any system is exploration of student concerns. Despite conflicts in other areas, the client-centered approach lends very well to the examination and exploration of the client's problems.

Client-centered counseling encourages the counselee to act only in response to dependable motives. Testing for trust depends in large measure on the depth of the client's concerns. Client-centered counseling affords the opportunity to explore the mutuality of trust.

The examination of feelings does not rule out planning for action. However, implementing plans evolves out of the insights gained rather than the listing of discrete unrelated goals. Of course, most students and parents want specific action—in fact, discrete action to improve or modify behavior.

Counselee–openness—The generally soft, gentle, slow-moving process of client-centered counseling allows a counselee with a deep concern to gain confidence in being open about his living. A key difficulty in implementing any counseling approach in the schools is that students are not familiar with it and do not know what to expect. The language of counseling is strange. This is particularly true for client-centered counseling since social sanctions usually forbid the expression of one's emotions.

Client-centered counseling does offer a "feeling" reward. However, specific rewards related to many school concerns are not readily evident.

Reality dimensions—The reality dimensions of time, ratio, sanctions, and school progress (getting into college) help work against the client-centered approach as a very usable way of counseling in schools.

References

(1) Allen, Thomas W. and John N. Whiteley, *Dimensions of Effective Counseling* (Columbus, Ohio: Charles E. Merrill Publishing Company, 1968).

(2) Armor, David, *The American School Counselor* (New York: The Russell Sage Foundation, 1969).

(3) Bischof, Ledford J., *Interpreting Personality Theories* (New York: Harper & Row, Publishers, 1964).

(4) Boy, Angelo V. and Gerald J. Pine, *The Counselor in the Schools—A Reconceptualization* (Boston: Houghton Mifflin Company, 1968).

(5) Coulson, William R., "Client-Centered Therapy and the Nature of Man," Ph.D. diss., University of Notre Dame, 1965.

(6) Dallis, Constantine A., "The Development of Rogerian Thought and Its Implications for Counselor Education," Vol. 3, Ph.D. diss., University of Wisconsin, 1965.

(7) Ford, Donald H. and Hugh B. Urban, *Systems of Psychotherapy: A Comparative Study* (New York: John Wiley & Sons, Inc., 1963).

(8) Gendlin, E. T., "Client-Centered Developments and Work with Schizophrenics," *Journal of Counseling Psychology, 9* (Fall, 1962), pp. 205–12.

(9) Gilliland, Burl E., "Small Group Counseling with Negro Adolescents in a Public High School," *Journal of Counseling Psychology, 15* (March, 1968), pp. 147–52.

(10) Hall, Calvin S. and Gardner Lindzey, *Theories of Personality* (New York: John Wiley & Sons, Inc., 1957).

(11) Hall, Mary Harrington, "A Conversation with Carl Rogers," *Psychology Today* (December, 1967), pp. 19–21, 62–66.

(12) Harper, Robert A., *Psychoanalysis and Psychotherapy: 36 Systems* (Englewood Cliffs, N.J.: Prentice-Hall, Inc., 1959).

(13) Hart, Joseph, "The Development of Client-Centered Therapy," in J. T. Hart and T. M. Tomlinson (eds.), *New Directions in Client-Centered Therapy* (Boston: Houghton Mifflin Company, 1970).

(14) Janis, Irving L. et al., *Personality: Dynamics, Development, and Assessment* (New York: Harcourt, Brace & World, Inc., 1969).

(15) Maddi, Salvatore R., *Personality Theories: A Comparative Analysis* (Homewood, Ill.: Dorsey Press, 1968).

(16) Mehrabian, Albert, *An Analysis of Personality Theories* (Englewood Cliffs, N.J.: Prentice-Hall, Inc., 1968).

(17) Moulin, Eugene K., "The Effects of Client-Centered Group Counseling Using Play Media on the Intelligence, Achievement, and Psycholinguistic Abilities of Underachieving Primary School Children," *Elementary School Guidance and Counseling, 5* (December, 1970), pp. 85–98.

(18) Patterson, C. H., *Theories of Counseling and Psychotherapy* (New York: Harper & Row, Publishers, 1966).

(19) _____ "A Current View of Client-Centered or Relationship Therapy," *The Counseling Psychologist, 1* (Summer, 1969), pp. 2–25.

(20) Pine, Gerald J., "The Effectiveness of Client-Centered Counseling in a Junior High School: Some General Findings," *Guidance Journal, 5* (Winter, 1967), pp. 91–95.

(21) Rogers, Carl R., *Clinical Treatment of the Problem Child* (Boston: Houghton Mifflin Company, 1939).

(22) _____ *Counseling and Psychotherapy: Newer Concepts in Practice* (Boston: Houghton Mifflin Company, 1942).

(23) _____ "Some Observations on the Organization of Personality," *American Psychologist, 2* (September, 1947), pp. 358–68.

(24) _____ *Client-Centered Therapy* (Boston: Houghton Mifflin Company, 1951).

(25) _____ "A Theory of Therapy, Personality, and Interpersonal Relationships, as Developed in the Client-Centered Framework," in Sigmund Koch (ed.), *Psychology: A Study of a Science* (New York: McGraw-Hill Book Company, 1959), Vol. 3, pp. 184–256.

(26) _____ *On Becoming a Person* (Boston: Houghton Mifflin Company, 1961).

(27) _____ "The Interpersonal Relationship: Core of Guidance," *Harvard Educational Review, 32*:4 (1962), pp. 416–29.

(28) _____ "The Therapeutic Relationship: Recent Theory and Research," *Australian Journal of Psychology, 17* (August, 1965), pp. 95–108.

(29) _____ (ed.) *The Therapeutic Relationship and Its Impacts: A Study of Psychotherapy with Schizophrenics* (Madison, Wisc.: University of Wisconsin Press, 1967).

(30) _____ *Freedom to Learn* (Columbus, Ohio: Charles E. Merrill Publishing Company, 1969).

(31) _____ "Nondirective Counseling: Client-Centered Therapy," in William S. Sahakian (ed.), *Psychotherapy and Counseling* (Chicago: Rand McNally & Company, 1969), pp. 169–209.

(32) _____ *Carl Rogers on Encounter Groups* (New York: Harper & Row, Publishers, 1970).

(33) Salomone, Paul R., "A Client-Centered Approach to Job Placement," *Vocational Guidance Quarterly, 19* (June, 1971), pp. 266–70.

(34) Snyder, William U. (ed.), *Casebook of Non-Directive Counseling* (Boston: Houghton Mifflin Company, 1947).

(35) Truax, Charles B., "Reinforcement and Nonreinforcement in Rogerian Psychotherapy," *Journal of Abnormal Psychology, 71*:1 (1966), pp. 1–9.

4 Developmental Counseling

INTRODUCTION

Developmental counseling is an essentially new approach or emphasis which has created much interest in the field of counseling and guidance. Not entirely unlike the eclecticism of some authors (9; 25), it is characterized somewhat by strong interdisciplinary undergirdings. Arbuckle has noted that in the literature of the last few years,

> by far the major impact has been related to the words 'developmental' and 'behavioral,' and this has reasonably come about as a result of the marked effect of the behavioral sciences in the whole area of learning and learning theory (2, p. 219).

In spite of this interest, little organization has come yet to the developmental counseling area. Zaccaria states:

> Developmental guidance has had a very brief history. Its entire past is limited to a few dozen books and journal articles which describe the various aspects of a process which has been largely theoretical, rather than actual. (28, p. 229).

Many writers have attempted to define developmental counseling, and some use the terms *counseling* and *guidance* synonymously. According to Shertzer and Peters, "Developmental guidance, and in particular developmental counseling, is primarily concerned with enhancing individuality within a framework of the larger social dimensions of behavior" (24, p. 37). A somewhat similar view is held by Blocher: "One basic assumption of developmental counseling is that human personality unfolds in terms of a largely healthy interaction between the growing organism and the culture or environment" (5, p. 4). A different but congruent approach is expressed by Zaccaria: "In the broadest sense, developmental guidance represents a change from crisis guidance toward a preventive and positive approach for helping pupils" (28, p. 226). Blocher shares this view, stating that "developmental counseling is concerned with developmental-educative-preventive goals, not remediative-adjustive-therapeutic outcomes" (5, p. 10).

The antecedents of developmental counseling would be difficult to trace. Many writers who have not concerned themselves with a strictly developmental framework have written in generally developmental terms. Some years ago Miller wrote of the interdisciplinary and developmental constructs of guidance and counseling (18). At about the same time Tyler wrote that the "psychological purpose of counseling is to facilitate development" (26, p. 17). Mathewson listed one of the major strategies of guidance as developmental, characterizing it as a process of pupil education through individual and group counseling and curricular experience for the purpose of preparing individuals to deal more capably with "self-situational relations" (17, p. 116).

Other writers, possibly eclectic, sound very much like developmental theorists. Thus, Mortensen and Schmuller write, "The primary goal of counseling is to help the counselee grow toward maturity" (20, p. 337). And Shostrom and Brammer, who are eclectic writers, cite their "emphasis upon this developmental or process approach to counseling" (25, p. 5). Likewise, Lister's article on the eclectic counselor also sounds very much like a description of a developmental counselor (16).

Developmental theory is a wine of recent vintage which takes grapes from many vines. Tyler has written how developmental theory borrows from theoretical sources (27). In a later text, Brammer and Shostrom confess their indebtedness. "The reader will note considerable 'borrowing' from other theories which have made unique and rich contributions" (9, p. 53).

There is no one author of the developmental theory. The best single work is Blocher's *Developmental Counseling* (5), along with three of his shorter writings which cover the developmental concepts rather well. Other works which have made contributions are: Shertzer and Peters, *Guidance: Techniques for Individual Appraisal* and *Development* (24); Peters and Farwell, *Guidance: A Developmental Approach* (23); Tyler, *The Work of the Counselor* (26); Dinkmeyer and Caldwell, *Developmental Counseling and Guidance in Elementary Schools* (13); Kell and Burow, *Developmental Counseling and Therapy* (15); and Peters, *The Guidance Process* (22).

BIOGRAPHICAL INFORMATION

The principal theorist of the developmental theory of counseling, Donald Hugh Blocher, was born August 7, 1928. He received his baccalaureate degree in 1950 and his master of arts degree in 1954 from Ball State Teachers College. In 1959 he was graduated from the University of Minnesota with a Ph.D. He has worked as a teacher and psychologist in various public school systems and was a rehabilitation counselor in a hospital at one time. He is currently in the Department of Educational Psychology at the University of Minnesota.

Other contributors to this theory have had somewhat similar backgrounds. Peters, Farwell, Shertzer, and Zaccaria have all had experience in public education at the elementary or secondary levels. These writers appear to have been influenced by their experiences in public education rather than by clinical or abnormal psychology.

PHILOSOPHY AND CONCEPTS

In describing developmental counseling Blocher has said:

It is possible within this point of view to conceive of an underlying discipline for counseling based upon the study of human effectiveness and organized around dimensions such as social roles, coping behavior, and developmental tasks (6, p. 732).

The first goal of developmental counseling is maximizing human freedom (5, p. 5); the second, maximizing human effectiveness (5, p. 6). These goals share the premise that while humans may, indeed, have very little freedom, few of them are prepared to exercise the freedom they do have (5, p. 5). Zaccaria agrees with these aims: "Behind the application of techniques is an objective—a positive goal of helping the individual to achieve maximum development in all aspects of his life" (28, p. 226). Shertzer and Peters see a slightly different goal, "the enhancement of an already adequately functioning person to new heights of achievement" (24, p. 38).

A number of basic assumptions concerning the nature of clients and counselors are important to the developmental counseling framework. These assumptions are summarized from Blocher (5, p. 11):

1. The clients are not to be thought of as mentally ill as the illness concept is largely inappropriate and irrelevant to a process focused on changing behavior.
2. The focus of counseling is on the present and future. Counselors are concerned with where the client is going, not where he has been.
3. The subject in the counseling interview is a client, not a patient. The counselor is essentially a teacher and partner of the client as he progresses toward mutually acceptable goals.
4. The counselor has values, standards, and feelings but does not necessarily impose them on his client.
5. The counselor focuses on the change of behavior, not just the enhancement of client insight.

It is necessary to understand the developmental model for conceptualizing the relationship between developmental counseling and its goal of maximizing human effectiveness. The model, adapted from Blocher, has four parts (5, pp. 6–9):

1. "Roles and Relationships." Individuals from birth to death are constantly in the process of entering new roles. "At each moment of life, any person is in process of changing into something a little different from what he now is" (27, p. 37). There are great differences among individuals as to how well they handle these role changes. Serious discontinuities can occur between developmental and environmental demands, and when they do, counseling is necessary.
2. "Coping Behaviors." The counselor should understand the wide range of coping behavior available to the client. He must help his client acquire new coping behaviors if the ones he has are inappropriate.
3. "Developmental Tasks." The facilitation of human development is largely dependent upon the individual's ability to master tasks that will equip him with the necessary coping behaviors. The developmental counselor must be an expert in

helping the individual understand and master the appropriate developmental tasks.
4. "Identity Formation: A Central Developmental Task." As used in the developmental framework, the construct of identity goes beyond the usual meaning of "self-concept." Identity formation implies the development of multiple self-concepts. It is the sense of belonging to and caring about other individuals, groups, and ideals. Identity formation is an active, ongoing process of interaction with the environment.

Because of the positive tenor of developmental counseling—emphasizing the growth of human effectiveness—it becomes more important for a counselor to know the stages of normal development than the stages of abnormal development.

Dinkmeyer cites much in child-development research that implies the need for developmental counseling with normal children (11; 10). He emphasizes that developmental counseling is based upon a continuing developmental framework or contract. The contract is based on counselee willingness to make a commitment to *process* in development. The process includes self-exploration, willingness to consider alternatives, and movement toward change (12).

Peters and Farwell (23) among others (9) also support the need to understand the developmental sequence. Five developmental stages are listed by Blocher (5, pp. 49–68):

1. "The Organization Stage" is characterized by the physiological unfolding of the organism. This stage is broken down into four substages: infancy (1–3), early childhood (3–6), later childhood (6–12), and early adolescence (12–14).
2. "The Exploration Stage" is characterized by a reaching out for new values, ideals, motivations, and purposes. This stage is broken down into two substages: later adolescence (15–19) and young adulthood (20–30).
3. "The Realization Stage" is characterized by a culmination of effective human development. Maturation physically and psychologically are set. This stage starts at 30 and runs to 50.
4. "The Stabilization Stage" is characterized by refinement of a high level of functioning. This stage starts at 50 and runs to or beyond age 65.
5. "Examination Stage" is characterized by reflection and active disengagement from events. The role of observer re-

places participant, and mentor replaces actor. This stage starts around 65.

In striving for the development of human effectiveness, the responsibility of the counselor, as seen by Shertzer and Peters, is (24, p. 39):

1. to assist each individual to understand and accept his potentials for living;
2. to assist the counselee to appraise periodically his developmental progress; and
3. to work with the counselee in planning his next phase of living.

Tyler sees the issue in a broader framework: "As I have considered this matter, the orientation I have found most helpful is to consider the whole developmental process as the actualization of potentialities" (27, p. 39). Blocher attempts to synthesize six models of human effectiveness into one model appropriate for developmental counseling. The model has five parts (5, pp. 80–83):

1. "Consistency." The effective person is reasonably consistent in his social and individual behavior.
2. "Commitment." The effective person is able to commit himself to selected goals and purposes reasonably without taking unnecessary risks.
3. "Control." The effective person is able to control his emotional responses. He is able to cope with frustration, ambiguity, and hostility.
4. "Competence." The effective person is an effective problem solver. He possesses a wide repertory of coping behaviors.
5. "Creativity." The effective person is able to think in divergent and original ways.

CONCEPTION OF MAN

The nature of man as postulated under the developmental framework is not clearly delineated. Blocher states that building a personal philosophy of counseling is a central task for the development counselor (5, p. 16). Many of the traditional philosophical positions are given in his book, but none of these positions receives any recommendations. The position taken by Shertzer and Peters seems closely allied to trait-factor theory:

> Nondirectivism, listening, catharsis, rapport-building, reassurance, and permissiveness may be misinterpreted by the nonpathological pupil as resounding approval for a mode of behavior far below what might reasonably be expected of him (24, p. 40).

On the other hand, a behaviorist note is sounded: "Reinforcement is the *sine qua non* factor in developmental counseling" (24, p. 41). Blocher attempts to synthesize the various philosophical systems by using a set of assumptions from Beck (3) that offer a useful basis for developmental counseling (5, p. 20):

1. Man is responsible for his own actions. He must make choices himself.
2. Man must regard his fellow men as worthwhile. He must be concerned with individuals as well as society.
3. Man must exist in a world, much of which he cannot change, but this is reality.
4. Man's life, to be meaningful, must be free from threat.
5. Man has his own unique experience and heredity.
6. Man acts in terms of his own subjective view of reality.
7. Man cannot be classified as either good or evil by nature as these terms more aptly apply to patterns of behavior.
8. Man reacts as a total organism.

Obviously, what Blocher judges as appropriate for a basic philosophy of developmental counseling is strongly existential.

RELATED THEORY OF PERSONALITY

Developmental counselors do not emphasize personality theory. Blocher calls it a "romantic if ephemeral will-o-wisp, which has succeeded only in translating the speculations of philosophy into the jargon of psychology" (8, p. 135). Arguing that personality theory is not beneficial to counseling, he maintains that the psychology of learning and social psychology have much more to offer counselors (8). Rather than emphasis on theory of personality, Blocher contends, an organized body of knowledge concerning the development of human effectiveness is needed for counselor education (6, p. 732).

Brammer and Shostrom have a broader view. "Although there is no theory of personality which is suitable to frame the practice of counseling and psychotherapy, each position has unique implications for practice" (9, p. 62). There is no reason to believe that all the major developmental writers would not borrow those elements from any theory of personality which fit their personal inclination and need.

THEORY OF THERAPY

There are essentially two types of treatment appropriate to developmental counseling—direct intervention, in which there is a direct relationship between the counselor and the client, and indirect intervention, in which the counselor attempts to utilize elements in the client's environment which can facilitate growth (7, p. 10). Both of these accommodate the theory of therapy as proposed by developmental writers.

PROCESS

The following characteristics of a developmental relationship are important to understanding the total theory (5, pp. 143–53):

1. "Congruence." This characteristic is concerned with the quality of being one's self. The opposite of this would be "phony," artificial behavior or the playing of some assumed role.
2. "Unconditional Positive Regard." This characteristic essentially means that the counselor has an interest in and concern for the client. He does not engage in moral judgments concerning the client.
3. "Empathic Understanding." This characteristic involves two components. One is a cognitive element that facilitates psychological understanding. The other is an affective element that involves feeling with the client.
4. "Trust." This dimension is based on an individual's feeling of certainty that he can predict another's behavior under a given set of circumstances.
5. "Limits." Every counseling relationship must have limits for both the counselor and the client: time, the nature of interaction, ethics, and so forth.
6. "Dependency." The counselor must accept this characteristic in a client without acceding to his demands for it. The counselor must help the client face and work through this need.
7. "Transference." At times within the counseling relationship, the client may develop irrational feelings of either a positive or negative nature toward the counselor or vice versa. These

feelings, known as transference, must be exposed and worked through.

8. "Resistance." This is the client's conscious or unconscious hindrance to progress in the counseling process.

Diagnosis in developmental counseling is based on the counselor's ability to understand the client, his world, and the meaning that this world interaction has for him (5, p. 130). Diagnosis is made with reference to the degree of control the client can exert over his environment, rather than the cause of a disorder or disease as in medical practice. In essence it is a rating of the client's ability to function at one of the five levels of human effectiveness which are listed below as summarized from Blocher (5, pp. 128–30):

1. "Panic." Panic is the loss of control over affective responses in the immediate or short-term environment. The individual may have intense feelings of being out of control, and in such a state he is usually institutionalized.
2. "Inertia." At this level of effectiveness the individual has some control over short-term immediate aspects of the environment, but little or no control over long-term aspects. He is unable to carry through plans that require organized, controlled behavior. He is not likely to be self-sufficient either economically or socially.
3. "Striving." The individual has some control over long-range aspects of his environment and is actively seeking more control. He is likely to alternate between feelings of hope and despair.
4. "Coping." The individual has control over large segments of his environment. His behavior is controlled and largely goal oriented. Anxiety does not extinguish appropriate risk-taking behavior.
5. "Mastery." Mastery is the highest level of human effectiveness. The individual is characteristically able to enter into planful interaction with his environment. He has a sense of adequacy and mastery in most roles. He is involved with a commitment to values that may transcend his own existence.

TECHNIQUES

Technique, which is as important to developmental counseling as process orientation, has been described by Shertzer and Peters as well as by Blocher. Both descriptions give a rounded picture of the interview and the technique employed. Following is a summary of eleven techniques which may be used in developmental counseling (24, pp. 42–49):

1. "Appraising." The counselor uses all the methods at his disposal to assist the client in appraising himself. These methods include the give-and-take of the counseling interview, questioning, test results, and diagrams. Here diagnosis is used to focus on the center of developmental action.
2. "Information-Giving." This involves the presentation of information when the counselee needs it.
3. "Encouraging." The counselor's wise use of encouragement becomes a significant factor in the client's "life space." Ego strength, it is postulated, can be built up by significant others.
4. "Planning." Planning is based on the counselor's knowledge of development, appraising, information-giving, and encouraging.
5. "Researching." The counselee must be an active participant in researching himself. He must become aware of his abilities, adequacies, and attitudes.
6. "Analyzing." The counselee's self-analysis is the crux of developmental counseling. The counselor assists in this search, but it is the counselee who must adequately perceive himself.
7. "Interpreting." Interpretation is the explanation of meanings gained from researching and analyzing.
8. "Clarifying." Clarification is used to pinpoint an exact meaning or to reorganize concepts. It is part of the interpreting process and may be used by either the counselee or the counselor.
9. "Approving." Responsible approval is used in developmental counseling to reinforce counselee choices toward positive action.
10. "Evaluating." Evaluation may be necessary when the counselee attempts to examine discrepancies between potential and performance or between inner needs and environmental pressures.
11. "Reinforcing." The developmental counselor reinforces strengths and successes in the counselee.

Blocher writes of techniques of interviewing rather than techniques of counseling to stress the importance of the communication between counselor and client. He emphasizes three techniques in particular (5, pp. 156–64):

1. "Formulation of Goals." The formulation of goals in developmental interviewing is a two-sided coin. On one side is the counselor's own personal theory and philosophy, and on the obverse, the client's self-perceptions. With the mutual formulation of goals comes the process of "structuring," the communicating and sharing of mutual expectations.
2. "Dimensions of the Counseling Process." There are three possible dimensions along which the counseling process may be structured.
   a. "Division of Responsibility." This is the assignment of responsibility to both the client and the counselor for the ongoing process of the interview.
   b. "Ambiguity." This refers to the degree of openness or uncertainty that exists in the minds of the client and/or counselor as to what is going to happen or be said next.
   c. "Affective-Intellectual Dimension." This dimension distinguishes purely emotional responses from purely cognitive or intellectual responses.
3. "Perceptual Skills." What the developmental counselor says is less important than his ability to listen. He must carefully develop this form of perception and become a total, not a selective, listener.

GOALS

The processes and techniques of developmental counseling or developmental interviewing lead to explicitly formulated goals:

1. "The fundamental goal of developmental counseling is the enhancement of an already adequately functioning person to new heights of achievement" (24, pp. 38–39).
2. Developmental counseling has the goal of maximizing human freedom (5, p. 5).
3. Developmental counseling has the goal of maximizing human effectiveness (5, p. 6).
4. Developmental counseling has the goal of congruence with the human effectiveness modes (5, pp. 80–83).

SUMMARY

Developmental counseling is an essentially new approach to counseling and is not totally unlike the eclectic empha-

sis of a few years ago. Although developmental counseling has ex-
cited interest, to date only a few dozen books and journal articles
about it have been published (2; 28). An even more limited amount
of research has been done (4).

Developmental counselors emphasize an educational setting
more than do many other counselors.

> The psychological purpose of counseling is to facilitate develop-
> ment. Thus it can be considered as part of the whole broad
> educational process that extends from the earliest months of
> infancy to the declining years of old age (26, p. 17).

Shertzer and Peters show this emphasis when they define the interests of the developmental counselor:

> He has a strong commitment in elementary and secondary edu-
> cation. He participates actively in elementary-secondary educa-
> tion professional circles. . . . He communicates with professional
> school colleagues in a way that is consistent with the total educa-
> tional program and the developmental concept—for example he
> says 'counselee' in place of 'client,' the clinical term. His profes-
> sional interest is primarily concerned with the guidance func-
> tion with the vast majority of pupils in the school setting (24, pp.
> 49–50).

In the broadest sense this view represents a shift from crisis
counseling toward a preventive and positive approach toward helping pupils (28, p. 10). Blocher holds a somewhat similar view when
he writes that developmental counseling is concerned with develop-
mental-educative and preventive goals rather than remediative-
adjustive and therapeutic outcomes (5, p. 10). Oetting has even
reconsidered the definition of counseling psychology, terming it the
"study of the mental health of individuals engaged in developmental
processes" (21, p. 382).

Shertzer and Peters characterize the developmental approach
as follows (24, pp. 40–41):

1. "Counselees." There is concern with those functioning normally as well as those who have problems.
2. "Counselor Initiative." The counselor should use his initiative in arranging interviews.
3. "Focus on Strengths." There is positive rather than negative
   focus in interviews.

4. "Purposeful Stimulation." There is purposeful injection of appropriate stimuli into the pupil's stream of behavior.
5. "Exploration for Action." Possibilities for using one's potential are examined.
6. "Analysis." There is mutual examination of choices and possible choices.
7. "Implementation." Choices are put into action.
8. "Reinforcement." There is selective emphasis of counselee ideas.
9. "Integration." All elements are fitted together into a cohesive relationship.

As a system, developmental counseling is tolerant of other theories and philosophies. "Each counselor must formulate a personal philosophy and theory of counseling if he is to really know himself" (18, p. 86). Blocher and Shertzer and Peters have "borrowed" widely from other theories. Peters and Farwell's book further emphasizes this integrative approach (23).

Whether the theory is really distinct or, as Arbuckle says, what appear to be differences in counseling are but differences in counselors (2), only time will tell. "But while developmental guidance is not a panacea, it constitutes an approach which is positive in its orientation in a time filled with neutralism and uncertainty" (28, p. 229).

SELECTED RESEARCH

Moore reports a developmental group counseling project with seventh graders (19). The project was initiated through fall orientation groups during which students discussed school and student characteristics associated with and occurring in the seventh grade. At the conclusion of each session, students completed questionnaires reflecting four categories of subjects for and attitudes toward counseling: (1) interpersonal skills, (2) study skills and school behaviors, (3) not interested, and (4) preference for individual or group counseling. Requests for individual counseling were followed up but were not included in the study. Assistance and consensus of teachers and administration in developing the group counseling plan resulted in twelve groups, five study groups and seven interpersonal relations groups. There were five all-boy groups, five all-girl groups, and two boy-and-girl groups. Ten of the twelve groups met one fifty-five minute period per week for four weeks; one girls' group met for eight weeks; and one boys' group met for thirteen weeks. At the last session of each group, each student completed an oral (taped) and a written evaluation which was based on a modified Semantic Differential three-point scale. Weights of +1, 0, or –1 were assigned to positive, neutral, or negative approximations of the adjectives given. Girls felt more positive about the interpersonal groups, and the boys tended to feel more positive about the study groups. The group averages toward counseling groups were all positive, and ranged from 3.4 to 7.0 (on a rating scale with 10 as maximum). The verbal responses were not statistically treated. Fifteen of the eighteen teachers were in favor of continuing the program in the following year with expansion of it to include eighth and ninth graders.

The author concluded that the developmental approach resulted in opportunities for all seventh graders to participate in group counseling with the additional advantage of getting the group counseling program underway much more easily and efficiently than a problem-centered method.

Benson and Blocher report successful results with use of a developmental counseling approach with twenty-eight low achieving boys nominated by teachers as needing assistance (4). All twenty-eight volunteered to participate. Twelve students were placed in a control group, twelve in the experimental group, and four in a reserve category. Treatment consisted of one fifty-five minute group session per week for eighteen weeks. The groups emphasized developmental "problems of school and grades," the basis on which the students were asked if they wished to participate. Therefore, in the last twelve sessions how-to-study films were shown, and various other help was offered to the group in study methods such as SQ3R (Survey, Question, Read, Recite, Review), concentration, homework, and preparation for tests. The first six sessions and the remainder of the time in the last sessions were devoted to structuring and discussion of problems of interpersonal relations, which included role playing of "authority" figures such as teachers, parents, and the principal. In addition, "feedback" to each group member about himself was encouraged.

Results of the experimental versus control group on the criterion variables indicated (1) increased grade point average, significant at the 0.02 level; (2) reduction of disciplinary referrals to the principal (ten for experimental and seventeen for the control), although not significant; and (3) reduction in the number of problems from pre/post S.R.A. Youth Inventory scores. Perhaps an overriding result was the school-staying behavior of the students in the experimental group, all of whom returned to school the subsequent year (compared to only 75 percent of the control group). Limitations of the study include small sample size and external validity problems.

IMPLICATIONS FOR SCHOOL COUNSELORS

Social sanction—Developmental counseling would come close to having social sanction in the school and community. This is especially true as it relates to educational and vocational goals. Also, it is positive in that it accentuates the potentialities of children and youth and rarely probes the depths of past, personal, or familial discomforts.

School press—The demands of the school system lend themselves to developmental counseling. Educational achievement, vocational development, and personal fulfillment become the face of developmental counseling from the early elementary school years through formal post-secondary school learning experiences.

Counselor fit—The counselor can be comfortable with developmental counseling. The goals fit into those of the immediate school program. Yet they do not obscure the fullness of the development of the pupil as a person.

Counselor-Pupil Ratio—Here difficulty arises. Most, if not all, pupils could benefit from developmental counseling. Thus, current pupil-counselor ratios are unrealistic. Of course, this unrealism really applies across the spectrum of counseling theories.

Counselor—Developmental counseling emphasizes positive attributes more than problems or concerns. The exploration of strengths is viewed as a way to bring limitations into improved or at least manageable perspectives.

References

(1) *American Psychological Association 1970 Directory* (Washington, D.C.: 1970).

(2) Arbuckle, Dugald S., "Kinds of Counseling: Meaningful or Meaningless," *Journal of Counseling Psychology, 14* (May, 1967), pp. 219–25.

(3) Beck, C.E., *Philosophical Foundations of Guidance* (Englewood Cliffs, N.J.: Prentice-Hall, Inc., 1963).

(4) Benson, Ronald L. and Donald H. Blocher, "Evaluation of Developmental Counseling with Groups of Low Achievers in a High School Setting," *School Counselor, 14* (March, 1967), pp. 215–20.

(5) Blocher, Donald H., *Developmental Counseling* (New York: Ronald Press Company, 1966).

(6) _____ "Wanted: A Science of Human Effectiveness," *Personnel and Guidance Journal, 44* (March, 1966), pp. 729–33.

(7) _____ "What Can Counseling Offer Clients? Implications for Selection," in John Whiteley (ed.), *Research in Counseling,* (Columbus, Ohio: Charles E. Merrill Publishing Company, 1967), pp. 5–35.

(8) _____ "Counselor Education: Facilitating the Development of a Helping Person," in Clyde A. Parker (ed.), *Counseling Theories and Counselor Education* (Boston: Houghton Mifflin Company, 1968), pp. 133–44.

(9) Brammer, Lawrence M. and Everett L. Shostrom, *Therapeutic Psychology: Fundamentals of Counseling and Psychotherapy* (Englewood Cliffs, N.J.: Prentice-Hall, Inc., 1960).

(10) Dinkmeyer, Don C., *Child Development: The Emerging Self* (Englewood Cliffs, N.J.: Prentice-Hall, Inc., 1965).

(11) _____ "Developmental Counseling in the Elementary School, *Personnel and Guidance Journal, 45* (November, 1966), pp. 262–66.

(12) _____ "Developmental Counseling: Rationale and Relationship," *The School Counselor, 18* (March, 1971), pp. 246–52.

(13) Dinkmeyer, Don C., and Charles E. Caldwell, *Developmental Counseling and Guidance in Elementary Schools* (New York: McGraw-Hill Book Company, 1970).

(14) Hipple, John, "Development of a Personal Philosophy and Theory of Counseling," *School Counselor, 16* (November, 1968), pp. 86–89.

(15) Kell, Bill L. and Josephine M. Burow, *Developmental Counseling and Therapy* (Boston: Houghton Mifflin Company, 1970).

(16) Lister, James L., "The Eclectic Counselor: An Explorer," *School Counselor, 14* (May, 1967), pp. 287–94.

(17) Mathewson, Robert Hendry, *Guidance Policy and Practice,* 3rd ed. (New York: Harper & Row, Publishers, 1962).

(18) Miller, Carroll H., *Foundations of Guidance* (New York: Harper & Row, Publishers, 1961).

(19) Moore, Lorraine, "A Developmental Approach to Group Counseling with Seventh Graders," *School Counselor, 16* (March, 1969), 272–76.

(20) Mortensen, Donald G. and Allen M. Schmuller, *Guidance in Today's Schools,* 2nd ed. (New York: John Wiley & Sons, Inc., 1966).

(21) Oetting, E. R., "Developmental Definition of Counseling Psychology," *Journal of Counseling Psychology, 14* (July, 1967), pp. 382–85.

(22) Peters, Herman J., *The Guidance Process* (Itasca, Ill.: F. E. Peacock Publishers, 1970).

(23) Peters, Herman J. and Gail F. Farwell, *Guidance: A Developmental Approach,* 2nd ed. (Chicago: Rand McNally & Company, 1967).

(24) Shertzer, Bruce and Herman J. Peters, *Guidance: Techniques for Individual Appraisal and Development* (New York: The Macmillan Company, 1965).

(25) Shostrom, Everett L. and Lawrence M. Brammer, *The Dynamics of the Counseling Process* (New York: McGraw-Hill Book Company, 1952).

(26) Tyler, Leona, *The Work of the Counselor,* 2nd ed. (New York: Appleton-Century-Crofts, 1961).

(27) _____ "Theoretical Principles Underlying the Counseling Process," in Ben N. Ard, Jr. (ed.), *Counseling and Psychotherapy* (Palo Alto, Calif.: Science and Behavior Books, 1966), pp. 32–41.

(28) Zaccaria, J.S., "Developmental Guidance: A Concept in Transition," *School Counselor, 13* (May, 1966), pp. 226–29.

5 Existential Therapy

INTRODUCTION

Existentialism, as it relates to counseling in the United States, is primarily a European product and is philosophical rather than psychological in its orientation (1, p. 37). As Strickland notes, "Not too long ago existentialism was considered an atheistic philosophy. Today many disciplines are considering the philosophy for its positive attributes" (40, p. 470).

Although there is no one existential theory, the term "existential psychotherapy" has been applied to approaches that are primarily concerned with understanding the client as he exists in his world (35). Neither existential philosophers nor psychotherapists have achieved unanimity of thought. In a sense, then, existentialism is a term applied to a loosely organized series of approaches rather than a single "school." Friedman has even written: "Existentialism is not a philosophy but a mood embracing a number of disparate philosophies, the differences between which are more basic than the temper which unites them" (10, p. 104). And Strickland avers:

> Existentialism is a school of thought that is concerned with the individual and his attempt to retain his identity, make his own choices, and provide his own self-direction. The reason for this very general definition is that there is no single philosophy of existentialism (40, p. 471).

The existential philosophers, upon which one psychotherapy rests, have had a great impact upon the world of thought. Sartre (39),

Heidegger (14), Kierkegaard (18), Jaspers (15), and Tillich (42) are existential philosophers, whether atheist or theist; their central beliefs have similarities and differences. Sartre holds that existentialism is a doctrine which makes human life possible and declares that every truth and action implies a human setting in a human subjectivity (39, p. 10). "There can be no other truth to take off from than this: I think, therefore I exist" (39, p. 15). Jaspers writes:

> Because existence is consciousness and I exist as consciousness, things exist for me only as objects of consciousness. Anything which exists for me must enter into consciousness. Consciousness as existence is the medium of everything (15, p. 115).

Heidegger's writings are concerned primarily with the concept of being, which is the central concept in his philosophical position. "The being that exists is man. Man alone exists. Rocks are, but they do not exist. Trees are, but they do not exist. . . . The existential nature of man is the reason why man can be conscious of them (13, p. 215).

From these and other philosophical existential positions, practicing counselors have become involved in the existentialist movement. In this country the major exponents of this movement are May, van Kaam, Moustakas and Frankl, although Frankl spends much time in Vienna and could be classified as a European therapist. The individual therapists exhibit the same disparity of views as do the philosophers. None of the present existential psychotherapeutic approaches are as yet very systematic, but there are some common aspects basic to all existential approaches to psychotherapy. These embrace the following themes (35, pp. 445–46).

1. Humans have as a distinctive characteristic *Dasein* (the being who is there). In addition, humans have the capacity to be conscious of themselves as well as of the events in the past and present that influence them. The conception of the future is another uniquely human characteristic. Man can thus make choices and decisions based upon these data as he sees them. Having the freedom to make these decisions, *he is responsible* for the decisions and the actions that these decisions produce.
2. The subject and the world are inseparable. Man lives not in the world of the self, but in three worlds concurrently: the *Umwelt* or biological world, the *Mitwelt* or world of other

persons with whom he shares mutual consciousness or awareness, and the *Eigenwelt* or world of self-identity.

3. A human is thus being. He is not fixed but is becoming, i.e., in a state of continual transition. Man is fulfilling his potentialities by participating with others. It is at this point that the significance of therapy can be seen as an encounter with another to facilitate becoming.

4. Being also implies *nonbeing*. Existentialists hold that *nonbeing* (death) is what gives life reality since, along with being, it is the one absolute fact of life. The same is true for some writers' use of *existence* and *nonexistence*. Man is conscious of the confrontation with nothingness and emptiness.

5. The threat of nonbeing is the source of existential anxiety and is considered as being present in all individuals. This anxiety can strike at the very core of an individual since it threatens the security and even dissolution of the self into nonexistence.

6. Each individual is unique and irreplaceable. He lives in *Eigenwelt* (his own world), in his self-identity. Each person is thus of ultimate significance.

7. Other than the limits of being, man has the capacity to transcend himself, to rise above the past and the present in a unique freedom to choose and become.

8. Man is characterized by alienation from the world. Loneliness and isolation are part of his existence.

Rollo May's works provide the best source for a discussion of existential therapy. Moustakas, Frankl, van Kaam, and Kemp provide additional information. The major offerings of these writers appropriate for our discussion are May, Angel, and Ellenberger's *Existence* (28); May's *Psychology and the Human Dilemma* (27); Moustakas' *Loneliness* (31) and *Existential Child Therapy* (33); van Kaam's *Existential Foundations of Psychology* (43); Frankl's *Man's Search for Meaning* (19); and Kemp's "Existential Counseling" (17).

BIOGRAPHICAL INFORMATION

Rollo May was born in Ada, Ohio, in April, 1909. He earned a baccalaureate degree at Oberlin College in 1930. From Oberlin he went to the American College in Salonika, Greece, to teach for three years. He then returned to Michigan State College in 1934 as a counselor, a position he held for two years before entering Union Theological Seminary. He was graduated from Union, cum laude, in 1938. In 1949 he received a Ph.D. degree in psychology from Columbia University.

While serving in private practice as a psychoanalyst much of his adult life, May also occupied posts on a number of faculties. Notable among these were the William Alanson White Institute of Psychiatry, Psychology, and Psychoanalysis (from 1948 to 1955 and from 1958 to present), the New School of Social Research (1955 to 1960), and New York University (1960 to present). In addition, he has had short tenures at Harvard, Yale, and Princeton. Currently he is supervisory and training analyst at the White Institute as well as adjunct professor at New York University. He is a fellow of the American Psychological Association.

During his years in Greece, May studied with Alfred Adler in Vienna each summer, and this experience led him indirectly into psychology. Later, while ill, he discovered the book that changed his life—Kierkegaard's *The Concept of Anxiety*. This led him to a degree in theology and ultimately a doctorate in psychology.

PHILOSOPHY AND CONCEPTS

Existential therapy has a linguistic base the root *ex-sistere,* which means, literally, to stand out or emerge. May explains: "Existentialism, in short, is the endeavor to understand man by cutting below the cleavage between subject and object which has bedeviled Western thought and science since shortly after the Renaissance" (28, p. 11).

Similarly Johnson has said: "By stressing existence, existentialism undercuts the dichotomy between subject and object. Man is not a subject who perceives an object, but exists with his objects" (16, p. 54).

In attempting to summarize existential concepts, Bates and Johnson have organized their thoughts around six essentials (3, pp. 245–49):

1. "Man's existence precedes essence." Man comes into the world from the unknown (birth) on the way to another unknown (death). The only thing that he knows is that he is.
2. "Man is condemned to freedom." Man is forced to make choices himself and, having made these choices, accept the full responsibility for them.

3. "When man chooses, he chooses for all men." Man in his lonely freedom is the only representative of mankind he will ever know.
4. "Man defines himself only through his actions." In man only action is relevant. Good intentions, what he says he will do or what he means to do, are irrelevant.
5. "The encounter—the 'I-Thou' relationship—defines counseling process and content." This bridge or connection between I and Thou forms the basis for the counseling relationship.
6. "Two worlds exist—the world of objective reality and the world of subjective reality." Man's world of objective reality is knowable. Subjective reality is only tentatively knowable.

Another way of examining the theory would be to look at the forces acting against existentialism. Looking at the counterindications makes the indications emerge with added clarity. May lists three sources of resistance to the existential movement (28, pp. 7–9):

1. All the important discoveries about psychotherapy have been made. We need only to fill in a few voids, not create a new system.
2. Existential thought is but an encroachment of philosophy into psychotherapy.
3. The preoccupation in this country with techniques rather than understanding.

The third criticism, or source of resistance, seems based on one of van Kaam's most important points: "Existential psychology demands that my potential data be observed as they exist before I attempt to interpret them" (43, p. 295). To these points Binswanger adds the caution of "overcoming our passionate need to draw conclusions, to form an opinion, or to pass judgment" (4, p. 192). The caution is meant to let the event or relationship speak for itself.

Ellenberger lists three concepts especially worthy of attention in understanding existentialist psychotherapy (6, pp. 119–20).

1. Existential neurosis arises from an individual's inability to grasp the meaning of life.
2. Existential therapists view the counseling relationship as an "encounter." The encounter is a decisive inner experience for one or both of the individuals involved.
3. Many existential therapists use the concept of *kairos* as the critical point when the patient is ready for therapy.

Moustakas has been particularly cognizant of the third point: "There is a time for crisis and a time of tranquility, a time of confrontation, and a time of encounter" (34, p. 5).

To these general philosophical concepts of existentialism Frankl adds a few others:

1. The primary force in man's life is his search for meaning (9, p. 154).
2. The meaning of man's existence is not invented by ourselves but detected (9, p. 157).
3. Pleasure is a side effect of experience, not its goal (9, p. 194).

The third of Frankl's points is perhaps more aptly stated by Kierkegaard: "The essence of pleasure does not lie in the thing enjoyed, but in the accompanying consciousness" (21, p. 51).

One other point basic to the understanding of existentialism has been stressed by both May (27) and Moustakas (32): The world attempts to put pressure on man to fit in and be significant in some group. This group significance is gained at the price of man's individual significance.

CONCEPTION OF MAN

May has proposed six essential characteristics which constitute the nature of an existing person (24):

1. Man is centered in himself. Neurosis is only one method the individual uses to protect his own center or existence.
2. Man has the character of self-affirmation, or the need to preserve his centeredness. The preservation of this centeredness takes will.
3. Man has the possibility of moving from centeredness to participation with other beings. The moving from centeredness to participation involves risk.
4. Awareness lies on the subjective side of man's centeredness. He is able to be subjectively aware of that with which he is in contact.
5. Man has a unique form of awareness called self-consciousness. Awareness means knowledge of external dangers and threats, and consciousness has to do with one's experience with himself as the subject who has a world.
6. Man has the characteristic of anxiety, the feeling of a man in a struggle against that which would destroy his being.

To these six characteristics Frankl would add a seventh.

7. The primary force in man's life is his search for meaning. Each man must have a unique and specific meaning, one that can be fulfilled by him alone. Man's striving toward existence takes will (9, pp. 154–71).

In an article on the new trend of existentialism some years ago, L. A. Pervin wrote: "The existential view of man, his uniqueness, his freedom, his responsibility, his own frame of reference, and will-to-meaning are worthy of serious attention and investigation" (36, p. 309).

RELATED THEORY OF PERSONALITY

The existentialist writers do not write of personality theory, and this can only be taken as a conscious omission rather than an oversight. This omission has not gone unnoticed in the literature. More than one writer has criticized existentialists for their lack of theory, rigor, and methodology (19; 36).

To the existentialist writers the conception of man seems to take on the role of personality theory. The existentialists only make statements about man which seem relevant in understanding man's travel from the unknown of birth to the unknown of death. They have fought the tendency to preface understanding with technique and have relied upon the opposite approach (23, p. 77).

Maslow has examined the existentialist movement and found it very enriching for psychology, even if it does not deal with a theory of personality (22). His statements on existentialism are even more useful to a careful evaluator. He starts by saying: "I am not an existentialist, nor am I even a careful and thorough student of this movement" (22, p. 52).

Although personality theory has been very important to most psychological theorists, the existentialists view it as irrelevant. They see man, at the present time, in a philosophical rather than a psychological light. Man in his existence is the only construct that holds relevance for them.

THEORY OF THERAPY

The existential approach to psychotherapy is not a system or a set of techniques, but is a concern with understanding man and his experience (26). "Those who read works on existential analysis as handbooks of technique are bound to be disappointed. They will not find specifically developed practical methods" (23, p. 76).

In spite of this warning by May, existential psychotherapists do have some common points when it comes to the process, techniques, and goals of therapy.

PROCESS

Various ideas from existentialist writers that relate to the process of therapy deserve attention.

1. Existentialism is an attitude in approaching other human beings. Like philosophy, it has to do with presuppositions underlying techniques (26).
2. "The central task and responsibility of the therapist is to seek to understand the patient as a being and as a being in his world" (23, pp. 76–77).
3. The therapist is committed to the "spontaneous, flowing, human processes and potentialities that are engendered and sparked in a communion of significant relationship" (33, p. 4).
4. "This process [of therapy] may enable the patient to create a world of meaning which is more congruent with his actual experience" (43, p. 106).
5. Diagnosis varies in importance among the existentialist writers. May and Moustakas do not stress it while Frankl and Binswanger do.
6. The "encounter," or the therapy session, is that which gives new meanings to life (6, p. 93).
7. There are no preconditions placed upon the clients by their therapists for entering into the encounter.
8. Therapy focuses on the future rather than the past (9, p. 152).

TECHNIQUES

Concepts of techniques can be abstracted from existentialist writers. May discusses six of crucial therapeutic importance (22, pp. 78–91):

1. Existential therapists evidence a wide variation in techniques employed. They vary from patient to patient and from phase to phase within treatment of an individual patient. Existential therapists sharply question the use of techniques simply because of custom. Existential techniques have flexibility and versatility.

2. Existential therapists realize that psychological forces take their meaning from the existential situation of the patient's immediate life. Each patient's behavior is seen and understood in the light of the existence of the patient as a human being.
3. Existential therapists emphasize "presence." The word "presence" means that the relationship of the patient and the therapist is taken as a real one. The therapist does not merely reflect but understands and experiences the patient.
4. Existential therapists will attempt to "analyze out" their ways of behaving that destroy presence. The therapist must not rely on technique to avoid confrontation.
5. Existential therapists aim therapy so that the patient will experience his existence as real. The patient must become aware of his potentialities and be able to act on them. Therapy is concerned with helping the person experience his existence.
6. Existential therapists attach a great deal of importance to commitment. Patients cannot get insight until they are ready to decide. A decisive attitude toward existence is an attitude of commitment. Knowledge and insight necessarily follow commitment.

Frankl adds to these techniques (9, pp. 193–204):

1. "Paradoxical intention." This technique requires the patient to intend that which he anticipates with fear. With this technique the patient can experience, at least for a short time, that which he has been fearing.
2. "De-reflection." This technique requires the patient to ignore the trouble and focus his attention on something else.

GOALS

The goals of therapy in the existentialist tradition are few and not handled in any great detail:

1. To make the client more aware of his existence (23).
2. To elucidate the client's uniqueness (5, p. 117).
3. To foster freedom in the client (44).
4. To improve the client's encounters with others (44).
5. To foster responsibility on the part of the client (23, p. 87).
6. To help the client establish his will to meaning (9, p. 154).

To these six goals Moustakas would add a seventh.

> The individual no longer gets in the way of himself; he knows
> what he wants; he is aware. It is this moment of awareness and
> discovery and presence that I call the existential moment; it is
> the moment when a person recognizes his own existence in the
> world and the unique and incomparable nature of that existence
> (33, pp. 1–2).

SUMMARY

Existentialism has been a relatively new psychotherapeutic development in the United States and remains inchoate.
It is not a system, and, with its strongly European philosophical
flavor, has been slow to achieve psychological respectability. One
reason has surely been its lack of methodological and experimental
rigor, traits which are highly valued in this country.

Existentialism has grown from work by the Danish philosopher
Kierkegaard (40, p. 470) and the German work *Sein und Zeit* by
Heidegger (20). European and American psychoanalysts have been
the first to incorporate existentialist thought into the therapeutic
relationship. More recently, other counselors have begun to embrace
these concepts.

The philosophy of existentialism has been viewed both widely
and divergently by those in the counseling profession. In the words
of Tiedeman, "The philosophy of existentialism argues the value
inherent in the right and the obligation of choosing while living" (41,
pp. 551–52). Or as Arbuckle has written: "Freedom of the individual
is considered to be the basic thread which permeates all views of
existentialism" (2, p. 558). Pine sounds a similar note. "The emphasis on freedom with accountability and the focus on man as the
creator of his culture and the master of his destiny make existentialism an attractive and dynamic philosophical force in counseling"
(37, p. 178).

On the other hand, Fontes stresses the understanding of man's
limitations: "One of the greatest contributions of existential philosophy has been its acceptance of the place of anxiety, guilt, and other
limiting factors, death included, as a part of the existence of man"
(8, p. 53).

Central to the practice of existential counseling are the following concepts. Humans have as a distinctive character *Dasein*. Man

and his worlds are inseparable. These worlds are *Umwelt* (biological), *Mitwelt* (others), and *Eigenwelt* (self). Man's character of *Dasein*, or, loosely, being, also involves nonbeing (death). It is this threat of nonbeing that produces anxiety, loneliness, and lack of will to meaning. Each human is unique and irreplaceable and has the capacity to transcend himself within the limits of his being.

The "encounter" is the mutual involvement of the counseling relationship. The I-Thou bridge in this relationship enables man to move toward understanding and meaning.

Man is viewed by most existentialists as neutral; that is, neither inherently good or bad. Without being saintly or evil, each man is, however, to be highly prized as he is a unique, irreplaceable entity.

Existentialists generally believe that understanding must emerge before technique. These therapists seem to feel that the emphasis on technique is an emphasis away from the encounter and therefore should be avoided. Maslow has commented upon this thesis, calling for a system of thought that rejects the physical, chemical, technological view of man (12). And, likewise, Landsman says of existentialism: "Perhaps its greatest promise is the increasing emphasis upon the self of the counselor and his enrichment in training rather than upon the mechanics of his technique" (19, p. 571).

In his critique, Friedman observes:

> Existential psychotherapy is faced, in the last analysis, with the same issue that faces all schools of psychotherapy: whether the starting point of therapy is to be found in the analytical category or the unique person in the construct of man or image of man (10, p. 117).

Existential therapists deal in the philosophical concepts of man's existence. Their terms are not like those customarily found in psychotherapy, and at times their writings sound almost poetic. Dreyfus explains, "If the existential terminology appears poetic, it may well be due to the poetic nature of man's being" (5, p. 117). Moustakas' work *Loneliness* represents both the theory and poetry of existentialism (31).

SELECTED RESEARCH

The search for research on existential counseling was difficult. The relationship to the school setting was equally difficult to find. Meltzoff and Kornreich indicate the paucity of research in existential therapy by making only one direct reference to research in their index (29). This research was not school-related but to the Mendel and Rapport study (30) on the effectiveness of the existential approach in treating chronic schizophrenic outpatients.

It is interesting to note that the major emphasis of *The Counseling Psychologist* in 1971 was on "Existential Counseling" (7). Research evidence was missing. The focus was on a dialogue of the meaning of living. The impact on counseling seemed incidental. Perhaps this illustrates again the difficulty in submitting existential counseling to a truly meaningful place in school counseling. Its very fine and exciting philosophy should not be confused with its implementation into guidance functions. Perhaps Carlton Beck was correct in saying that "it [existential counseling] could be criticized by many as 'mere poetry.' " In this issue (1971) he says, "Ten years later I see no reason to revise these estimates" (7, p. 1).

IMPLICATIONS FOR SCHOOL COUNSELORS

1. *Social sanction*—Because existentialist counseling has not been fully explored in the school, it is difficult to assess its social sanction. The idea that each person has dignity and worth because he exists and is a free being would certainly be sanctioned by school counselors and parents. The gray area for sanctions comes when emphasis is given to the individual to define himself and take full responsibility for his existence. The interpretation of this position is crucial. If parents interpret it as license to do as one pleases, there is doubt of their sanction.

2. *School press*—Existential counseling strives to enhance the pupil's freedom, improve his relationship with others, and assist the pupil in understanding his purposes. The acceptability of these aims within the school environment certainly varies from school to school.

3. *Counselor fit*—Some school counselors might be quite uneasy with existential counseling. The emphasis on a person-to-person, intensely human relationship might well be uncomfortable for a counselor who was not already an existentialist.

4. *Counselor-pupil ratio*—If the school counselor is to have intensive cognitive and emotional contact with the counselee, the nation's usual 1:250 or 1:300 ratio does not make sense. The time

necessary for this kind of experiencing would certainly necessitate a more favorable ratio.

5. *Counselor*—The existential counselor would certainly fit in comfortably with (a) exploring the counselee's concerns, (b) seeking his real motives, and (c) being at ease in a mutual trusting relationship. Out of this could emerge a genuineness in assisting the counselee in planning action. In existential counseling, the school counselor participates fully in experiencing the counselee's concerns. It is not merely a verbal exchange with the person called the "counselor." Non-verbal and subtle areas, subliminal language, and sensitive responses enhance existential participation.

6. *Counselee*—Existential counseling lends itself to openness. The student who is using psychic energy to defend himself can not be very open. But in an atmosphere of mutuality he can be open, and then he is free to change. Of course, "shaping" to the openness of existential counseling would probably be difficult for any students who have become distrustful of school in the past.

It would be difficult for the student living in a "now" world to perceive the immediacy of reward from existential counseling. The school counselor would have the counselee interpret his (the counselee's) evaluation of the worthwhileness of his immediate experiencing.

7. *Reality dimensions*—Time would be a crucial factor in existential counseling. Time is necessary to explore one's opportunities for and use of freedom. Because there is more concern for the total person than immediate problems, there would be emphasis on life style. The counselor is pointing out that it is the counselee as an individual who is important, his experience is the tests, and it is the realization that makes living significant or not so.

References

(1) Arbuckle, Dugald S., *Counseling: Philosophy, Theory and Practice* (Boston: Allyn and Bacon, Inc., 1965).

(2) _____ "Existentialism in Counseling: The Humanist View," *Personnel and Guidance Journal, 43* (February, 1965), pp. 558–67.

(3) Bates, Marilyn and Charles D. Johnson, "The Existentialist Counselor at Work," *School Counselor, 16* (March, 1969), pp. 245–50.

(4) Binswanger, Ludwig, "The Existential Analysis School of Thought," E. Angel (tr.), in R. May, E. Angel, and H. Ellenberger (eds.), *Existence: A New Dimension in Psychiatry and Psychology* (New York: Basic Books, Inc., Publishers, 1958), pp. 191–214.

(5) Dreyfus, Edward A., "The Counselor and Existentialism," *Personnel and Guidance Journal, 43* (October, 1964), pp. 114–17.

(6) Ellenberger, Henri, "A Clinical Introduction to Psychiatric Phenomenology and Existential Analysis," in R. May, E. Angel, and H. Ellenberger (eds.), *Existence: A New Dimension in Psychiatry and Psychology* (New York: Basic Books, Inc., Publishers, 1958), pp. 92–124.

(7) "Existential Counseling," *The Counseling Psychologist, 2:*3 (1971), pp. 1–60.

(8) Fontes, M. Emmanuel, *Existentialism and Its Implications for Counseling,* Synthesis series (Chicago: Franciscan Herald Press, 1965).

(9) Frankl, Viktor E., *Man's Search for Meaning: An Introduction to Logotherapy* (New York: Washington Square Press, 1959).

(10) Friedman, Maurice, "Existential Psychotherapy and the Image of Man," *Journal of Humanistic Psychology, 4* (Fall, 1964), pp. 104–17.

(11) Hall, Mary Harrington, "An Interview with 'Mr. Humanist,' Rollo May," *Psychology Today, 1* (September, 1967), pp. 25–29, 72–73.

(12) ———— "A Conversation with Abraham H. Maslow," *Psychology Today, 2* (July, 1968), pp. 35–37, 54–57.

(13) Heidegger, Martin, "The Way Back into the Ground of Metaphysics," in Walter Kaufmann (tr., ed.), *Existentialism from Dostoevsky to Sartre* (New York: Meridian Books, 1956), pp. 206–21.

(14) ———— *Being and Time*, J. Macquarrie and E. Robinson (trs.) (London: S. C. M. Press, 1962).

(15) Jaspers, Karl, "Communication through Transcendence," R. F. Grabau (tr.), in George Alfred Schrader, Jr. (ed.), *Existential Philosophers: Kierkegaard to Merleau Ponty* (New York: McGraw-Hill Book Company, 1967), pp. 109–60.

(16) Johnson, Ernest L., "Existentialism, Self-Theory and the Existential Self," *Personnel and Guidance Journal, 46* (September, 1967), pp. 53–58.

(17) Kemp, C. Gratton, "Existential Counseling," *The Counseling Psychologist, 2:*3 (1971), pp. 2–30.

(18) Kierkegaard, Søren, *Philosophical Fragments,* D. F. Swenson (tr.) (Princeton, N.J.: Princeton University Press, 1962).

(19) Landsman, Ted, "Existentialism in Counseling: The Scientific View," *Personnel and Guidance Journal, 43* (February, 1965), pp. 568–73.

(20) Lyons, J., "Existential Psychology: Fact, Hope, Fiction," *Journal of Abnormal and Social Psychology, 42* (March, 1961), pp. 242–49.

(21) Mackey, Louis H., "Søren Kierkegaard: The Poetry of Inwardness," in George Alfred Schrader (ed.), *Existential Philosophers: Kierkegaard to Merleau Ponty* (New York: McGraw-Hill Book Company, 1967), pp. 45–107.

(22) Maslow, Abraham H., "Existential Psychology–What's in it for Us?" in Rollo May (ed.), *Existential Psychology* (New York, Random House, 1961), pp. 52–60.

(23) May, Rollo, "Contributions of Existential Psychotherapy," in R. May, E. Angel, and H. Ellenberger (eds.), *Existence: A New Dimension in Psychiatry and Psychology* (New York: Basic Books, Inc., Publishers, 1958), pp. 37–91.

(24) _____ "Existential Bases of Psychotherapy," in R. May (ed.), *Existential Psychology* (New York: Random House, Inc., 1961), pp. 75–84.

(25) _____ (ed.), *Existential Psychology* (New York: Random House, Inc., 1961).

(26) _____ "Dangers in the Relation of Existentialism to Psychotherapy," in H. M. Ruitenbeck (ed.), *Psychoanalysis and Existential Philosophy* (New York: E. P. Dutton & Co., Inc., 1962), pp. 179–84.

(27) _____ *Psychology and the Human Dilemma* (Princeton, N.J.: D. Van Nostrand Co., 1967).

(28) May, Rollo, Ernest Angel, and Henri Ellenberger (eds.), *Existence: A New Dimension in Psychiatry and Psychology* (New York: Basic Books, Inc., Publishers, 1958).

(29) Meltzoff, Julian and Melner Kornreich, *Research in Psychotherapy* (New York: Atherton Press, Inc., 1970).

(30) Mendel, W. M., and Rapport, "Outpatient Treatment for Chronic Schizophrenic Patients: Therapeutic Consequences of an Existential View," *Archives of General Psychiatry, 8* (1963), pp. 190–96.

(31) Moustakas, Clark E., *Loneliness* (Englewood Cliffs, N.J.: Prentice-Hall, Inc., Spectrum Books, 1961).

(32) _____ *The Authentic Teacher* (Cambridge, Mass.: Howard A. Doyle Publishing Co., 1966).

(33) _____ *Existential Child Therapy: The Child's Discovery of Himself* (New York: Basic Books, Inc., Publishers, 1966).

(34) _____ "The Existential Movement," in Clark Moustakas (ed.), *Existential Child Therapy: The Child's Discovery of Himself,* (New York: Basic Books, Inc., Publishers, 1966), pp. 1–7.

(35) Patterson, C. H., *Theories of Counseling and Psychotherapy* (New York: Harper & Row, Publishers, 1966).

(36) Pervin, L. A., "Existentialism, Psychology, and Psychotherapy," *American Psychologist, 15* (1960), pp. 305–9.

(37) Pine, Gerald J., "Existential Counseling in the Schools," *School Counselor, 16* (January, 1969), pp. 174–78.

(38) Sahakian, William S. (ed.), *Psychotherapy and Counseling: Studies in Technique* (Chicago: Rand McNally & Company, 1969).

(39) Sartre, Jean-Paul, *Existentialism and Human Emotions,* B. Frechtman and H. E. Barnes (trs.) (New York: Philosophical Library, 1957).

(40) Strickland, Ben, "Kierkegaard and Counseling for Individuality," *Personnel and Guidance Journal, 44* (January, 1966), pp. 470–74.

(41) Tiedeman, David V., "A Symposium on Existentialism in Counseling: Prologue," *Personnel and Guidance Journal, 43* (February, 1965), pp. 551–52.

(42) Tillich, Paul, *The Courage to Be* (New Haven: Yale University Press, 1952).

(43) Van Kaam, Adrian, *Existential Foundations of Psychology* (Pittsburgh: Duquesne University Press, 1966).

(44) Vaughan, Richard P., "Existentialism in Counseling: A Religious View," *Personnel and Guidance Journal, 43* (February, 1965), pp. 553–57.

6 Behavioral Counseling

INTRODUCTION

Like existential therapy, behavioral counseling is a new approach to counseling based on old theory, in this case a learning theory called behaviorism. Fletcher states, "Nothing completely new has been added in the behavioral counseling development. Rather it is a new emphasis, giving the environment, along with learning and conditioning theory, proper attention" (14, p. 62).

Even though the procedures and theories used are not new, an intensified interest in this learning theory has come about in recent years.

> In the last few years, more specific kinds of counseling have been described in the literature, but by far the major impact has been related to words 'developmental' and 'behavioral,' and this has reasonably come about as a result of the marked effect of the behavioral sciences in the whole area of learning and learning theory (4, p. 219).

According to Hans Eysenck, "Behavior therapy is based on applying fundamental discoveries gained in the laboratory to practical problems" (13, p. 47). Michael and Meyerson identify the concept even further:

> A behavioral approach to counseling and guidance does not consist of a bag of tricks to be applied mechanically for the purpose of coercing unwilling people. It is part of a highly technical

system, based on laboratory investigations of the phenomena of conditioning, for describing behavior and specifying the conditions under which it is acquired, maintained, and eliminated (29, p. 382).

The influence of learning theory can easily be seen in the description above of behavioral counseling. As Breger and McGaugh have noted, behavioral techniques in therapy have been "encapsulated in a dogmatic 'school' " (8, p. 338). This encapsulation may not be instructive, however, since it does not allow for any clearer understanding of the concepts of behavioral counseling. Goodstein cautions, "There is no single behavior-theoretical view of counseling or psychotherapy but rather there are a number of such views" (15, p. 153). It is difficult, however, to identify these views.

Goodstein distinguishes two groups of behavior theorists. The first (Shoben, Dollard and Miller, Murray) uses procedures and techniques typical of rather traditional, psychoanalytical oriented approaches to counseling and psychotherapy.

The second (Wolpe, Eysenck, and Bandura) advocates direct intervention in manipulating the client's behavior (15, p. 154). Murray divides the theorists into the classical conditioning group (biotropic) which includes Eysenck, Salter, Shaw and Wolpe; and the social learning group (sociotropic) with Mowrer, Shoben, Murray, Dollard and Miller (31). Breger and McGaugh identify three positions associated with behaviorism or learning theory: (1) Dollard and Miller, (2) Eysenck and Wolpe, and (3) Skinner (8). Shertzer and Stone, two more educationally oriented writers, lump behavioral counselors into but one group, which includes Krumboltz, Thoresen, Bijou, Michael and Meyerson (34, p. 265). There are even differences among the theorists themselves as to their methods and interpretations. "Complete unanimity of approach to theory and technique is not to be found in any school of psychotherapy, and behavior therapists are no exception" (22, p. 260).

The major proponents of the behavioral counseling theory and their major works are H. J. Eysenck, *Behavior Therapy and the Neuroses* (11); John D. Krumboltz, *Revolution in Counseling* (26); Halmuth H. Schaefer and Patrick L. Martin, *Behavioral Therapy* (33); B. F. Skinner, *Science and Human Behavior* (37); and Joseph Wolpe and Arnold A. Lazarus, *Behavior Therapy Techniques* (46).

BIOGRAPHICAL INFORMATION

The writers selected for examination have diverse backgrounds. Three of them were educated out of the United States. One is a medical doctor; one is a counselor educator; and the rest are psychologists. However, they are all interested in conditioning and behavioral modification in the classical conditioning tradition exemplified by the work of Mary Cover Jones, working under J. B. Watson, in 1924 (19). A brief sketch of each of the major contributors of behavioral therapy follows.

Hans Jurgen Eysenck was born in 1916 in England. He was educated in the United Kingdom and attended the University of London, graduating with a Ph.D. in 1940. His interests and writings in the field of psychology have been prolific since 1940. Much of his work and interest has been in the field of psychometrics and personality. He has published two notable tests, namely, *The Maudsley Personality Inventory* and the more recent *Eysenck Personality Inventory*. He has written extensively in the area of behavioral modification and therapy, achieving much popular as well as professional recognition in the western world. Currently he is employed at the Institute of Psychiatry at Maudsley Hospital in London (11).

John Dwight Krumboltz, born in 1928, earned his Ph.D. in 1955 at the University of Minnesota. His interests are counseling behavior and research. He is in the School of Education, Stanford University.

Halmuth Hans Schaefer was also born in 1928 and received his Ph.D. thirty years later at the University of Chicago. He is currently employed as Research Psychologist at Patton State Hospital in Highland, California, where he works in behavioral counseling.

Patrick L. Martin, Ph.D., is a staff psychologist associated with the Patton State Hospital.

Burrhus Frederic Skinner has been the most prolific writer among the behaviorists. He was born in 1904 and attended Hamilton College in Clinton, New York, where his undergraduate experience pointed him to a career as a writer. After graduation he tried his skills in Greenwich Village, attaining "unnotable" success. Skinner then attended Harvard University where he received a Ph.D. in psychology in 1931 (16). Skinner has worked and written in the Pavlovian tradition and is most noted for his contributions in conditioning, scientific method, and animal experimentation. His operant conditioning apparatus has become widely known as the "Skinner Box," and he has been credited with much of the development of the teaching machine. Skinner's work has provided background material for behavioral counselors, with his contributions more theoretical than pragmatic. Currently professor of psychology at Harvard University, Skinner would not consider himself a practicing therapist.

Born in 1915 and educated in the Union of South Africa, Joseph Wolpe was graduated in psychiatry from the University of Witwateosrand with an M.D. degree. Today he is professor of psychiatry at Temple University.

Arnold A. Lazarus, Ph.D., also a South African, collaborated with Wolpe in his most recent book while employed at the Pennsylvania Psychological Institute in Philadelphia.

All of these writers have had experience working as psychologists and all of them have expressed interests in behavioral conditioning and research.

PHILOSOPHY AND CONCEPTS

"The word behavior has become such common coin that like all common coins it is shiny but faceless" (33, p. 3). So state Schaefer and Martin, remarking further that behavior is simply what an organism does, and therapy is any set of procedures which produce a beneficial change in a person. According to this definition, behavioral therapy is simply a process which produces beneficial changes in an organism. Skinner says, "Behaviorism is not the scientific study of behavior but a philosophy of science concerned with the subject matter and methods of psychology" (38, p. 79). Krumboltz has modified a definition of counseling to fit behavioral therapy. "Counseling consists of whatever ethical activities a counselor undertakes in an effort to help the client engage in those types of behavior which will lead to a resolution of the client's problems" (23, p. 384).

The deterministic instrumental aspects of behavioral therapy can be seen in many of the writers. Kanfer writes that some day psychotherapists may be able to offer two types of service: (1) "behavioral therapy" for socially crippling disorders, and (2) "friendship therapy" for the guidance of confused but generally socially adequate people (20). Bijou says,

> Instead of conceiving of the counselor as a reflector of feelings, or an explorer of resources, or a habit changer, or a remediator

of self-concepts and values, or a releaser of repressions, we might come to think of him as a behavioral engineer—one whose function it is to arrange and rearrange the environment in order to bring about desired changes in behavior (7, p. 44).

In addition to Bijou, both Kanfer (20) and Shoben (36) use the concept of behavioral engineering.

The diversity of approaches of behavioral counselors make any summary of ideas difficult. Thoresen's award-winning research did, in spite of the difficulties, produce a five-part characterization of behavioral counseling. The following points are paraphrased and summarized from his work (39):

1. Most human behavior is learned. The individual's environment is very influential in this learning. Since behavior is learned, it is subject to change.
2. With any change in environment may come a change in relevant behavior. Counseling procedures therefore attempt to change behavior by changing the client's environment.
3. Behavioral counseling does not rely on any single set of procedures, but social modeling and reinforcement usually play a major part in the process.
4. Only changes in client behavior outside the counseling interview are important in judging success or outcome.
5. Counseling procedures are designed to help a client solve the particular problem he brings to the interview. Techniques vary with the problem.

Behavioral therapists have developed many terms not wholly familiar to the psychotherapeutic community. Their vocabulary has been based, for the most part, on various learning theories. An examination of some of the more common terms may be instructive. The terms defined here are those most used by the behavioral theorists under consideration. Definition of a term by a particular writer, then, means the term is private to that writer, although these terms have almost universal use among the behavioral therapists. The choice of definitions is based on this paradox, their privacy and ubiquity.

1. "Aversion Therapy." The link between the conditioned stimulus and the pleasant response is broken by linking the response to an unpleasant experience (13, p. 46).

2. "Classical Conditioning." A new stimulus is associated or connected with a response which is normally precipitated by another stimulus.

3. "Counterconditioning." Strong responses which are incompatible with anxiety reaction can be made to happen in the presence of cues which evoke this anxiety. The incompatible responses will become attached to these cues and weaken the anxiety response (5, p. 97).

4. "Deprivation." Deprivation is the time a reinforcer is held from the organism. An example would be depriving a rat of food pellets (33, p. 30).

5. "Desensitization Therapy." The link between the conditional stimulus and the unpleasant conditional response is replaced by a new link between the conditional stimulus and a pleasant response. Desensitization therapy is the opposite of Aversion therapy (13, p. 46).

6. "Discrimination." Discrimination is the ability of the organism to select stimuli for response (33, p. 41).

7. "Experimental Extinction." This is the lessening or weakening of a habit through repeated non-reinforcement of the responses that manifest it (46, p. 14).

8. "Operant Conditioning." Spontaneous behavior is strengthened by reinforcement or weakened by negative reinforcement.

9. "Reciprocal Inhibition." This is Wolpe's term which parallels the concept of counterconditioning (45, p. 71).

10. "Reinforcement." A result or reward is designed to make a behavior (1) *more* likely to occur under similar conditions in the future (positive reinforcement), or (2) *less* likely to occur under similar conditions in the future (negative reinforcement) (29, p. 384).

11. "Shaping." A desired trait or action is selectively reinforced (29, p. 385).

Some other general concepts held by behavioral therapists are worthy of consideration. Eysenck says that neurotic symptoms are learned, and accordingly there are no neuroses which cause symptoms. There are only symptoms (13, p. 45). "Get rid of the symptoms and you have eliminated the neurosis" (12, p. 9). Skinner is even more emphatic: "A psychotic patient is psychotic because of his behavior. You don't institutionalize a person because of his feelings"

(10, p. 42). Bandura also states that idiosyncratic behavior is learned rather than physiologically produced (6, p. 61).

The behavior therapists have been concerned with how the patient learns (9, p. 89). The why has not been as important. This concern has been helpful in minimizing the number of constructs with which the therapist must deal as well as simplifying research. The "vital message is that there is no significant learning without action" (9, p. 93).

CONCEPTION OF MAN

To behavioral counselors and learning theorists in general, man is neither good nor bad. He is essentially neutral at birth, with equal potential for good or evil. "The behavioral technique is not tied to any assumption about the basic nature of man. From this view man has equal potential for good and evil" (9, p. 100). And Wrenn has written:

> For Skinner (or any behaviorist, I suppose) a man operates in computer fashion in which the output of results is determined by the input of signals. Life may design the program, or parts of it may be designed by a knowing operator in the life of man. But the computer has no autonomy—Skinner said this clearly at Duluth. Rogers (or any perceptual psychologist) would add the construct of a self which may also provide signals that will determine output. There is an intervening variable between receptor and effector and this has form and consistency. To Rogers this construct is essential to an understanding of at least adult behavior. To Skinner such a construct is a temporary expedient for those who find it necessary, but he finds it wholly unnecessary (49, pp. 101–2).

RELATED THEORY OF PERSONALITY

Behavioral therapy has been based on learning theory (32; 44). Unfortunately for the evaluation of behavioral therapy, there is no single theory of learning. The problem is even more confounded because few behavioral writers mention a specific learning theory. Krumboltz states a preference for Shoben's theory (25, p. 5), but Shoben favors a "two-factor learning theory of the type most recently developed by Mowrer" (35, p. 75). Two other writers have said that Murray's and Mowrer's theories are most appropriate (9, p. 89).

After examination of the behavioral therapy writers, a two-factor learning theory appears to describe the requirements of all of the theorists from the more biotropic (Eysenck-Wolpe-Skinner) to the sociotropic (Shoben-Krumboltz). Skinner's learning theory is also a two-factor theory (18, p. 64).

Mowrer's two-factor theory essentially reveals this theory's appropriateness to behavioral counseling (30). The two factors of the theory are punishment and reward. Mowrer calls punishment "incremental reinforcement" and reward "decremental reinforcement." Primary and secondary reinforcement are part of both incremental and decremental reinforcement. Secondary reinforcement is considered by Mowrer to be like the general concept incentive or hope. Primary reinforcement remains, as in other theories, direct strengthening of a response, whether positive or negative.

A basic outline of the present version of Mowrer's two-factor theory may be helpful (30, p. 213):

Incremental reinforcement (punishment)	Decremental reinforcement (reward)
A. Primary reinforcement	A. Primary reinforcement
B. Secondary reinforcement (incentive)	B. Secondary reinforcement (incentive)
C. Danger signal *on* (fear)	C. Danger signal *off* (relief)
D. Safety signal *off* (disappointment)	D. Safety signal *on* (hope)

> Revised two-factor theory assumes that so-called habit formation involves a strengthening of synapses between the neurones connecting stimuli produced by some behavioral act and the emotion of hope and that punishment involves a similar condition of fear (30, p. 220).

This discussion is not intended to be a complete statement of Mowrer's theory, but only a summary of the salient points as they relate to behavioral therapy.

THEORY OF THERAPY

Behavioral counseling is not a single theoretical view of psychotherapy. It is a number of such views (15). Writers tend to describe behavioral counseling in their individual ways, like blind men describing an elephant; but a whole animal can be created from the separate elements.

PROCESS

Krumboltz lists three conditions to the counseling process (23, p. 385). These conditions have to do with the limitations counselors might apply to their relationship with clients. The first condition has to do with the "interests" of the counselor. It is the counselor who must decide just what types of problems he is interested in helping to solve. The second limitation or condition has to do with "competency." The counselor must make clear to his client the limits of his competency. The counselor, as a third condition, must also evaluate the client's requests in terms of his own ethical standards.

The following processes seem to behavioral writers to be essential.

1. There is a "lifting of repression and development of insight through the symbolic reinstating of the stimuli for anxiety" (35, p. 75).
2. There is a "diminution of anxiety by counterconditioning through the attachment of the stimuli for anxiety to the comfort reaction made to the therapeutic relationship" (35, p. 75).
3. There is a "process of re-education through the therapists helping the patient formulate goals and behavioral methods for attaining them" (35, p. 75).
4. Diagnosis should pertain only to the functions of the client, not his traits (7, p. 44).
5. Symptoms have no underlying illnesses. There are only symptoms. Remove the symptom and you eliminate the disorder (13, p. 45; 10, p. 42).
6. "Most human behavior is learned and is therefore subject to change" (39, p. 17).
7. "The behavior therapist must be willing to dictate the procedures and direction of therapy" (9, p. 91).
8. The counseling process is a learning process (25, pp. 6–8).

TECHNIQUES

The processes of behavioral counseling are implemented by behavioral techniques, which are based on learning theory as found in many different sources:

1. Experimental extinction. The progressive weakening of a habit (46, pp. 14–15).

2. Counterconditioning or reciprocal inhibition. The pairing of a nonanxiety producing stimulus with an anxiety producing one to weaken the latter (46, p. 12).
3. Positive reconditioning. The conditioning of new motor habits or ways of thinking (46, p. 13).
4. Desensitization. The suppression of anxiety-producing stimuli (similar to counterconditioning) (33, p. 53).
5. Social modeling. The use of others as behavioral models (39, p. 69).
6. Contingency management. Behavior is largely determined by its consequences. By controlling consequences, some behaviors can be encouraged while others are discouraged or eliminated (40, p. 846).
7. Cognitive learning. Simply giving a client the information he needs (25, p. 16).
8. Aversive stimulation. An aversive outcome is an unpleasant outcome. This is similar to negative reinforcement and punishment (33, pp. 32–33).

GOALS

The process of therapy is implemented by the techniques of therapy in movement toward the therapeutic goals. The various goals of behavioral therapy, like the processes and techniques, come from many sources:

1. The alteration of maladaptive behavior in the client under therapy (25, p. 10).
2. The learning of a more efficient decision-making process (25, p. 11).
3. The prevention of future problems (25, p. 12).
4. The solution of the specific behavioral problem stated by the client. Counseling is based upon the requests of the client (23; 24).
5. Therapy must translate itself into action in life to be worthwhile (9, p. 87).
6. The specific and systematic base of therapy reduces ambiguity (9, p. 101).

The goals of counseling are capable of being stated differently for each client (24, p. 53).

SUMMARY

Behavioral therapy has been freely discussed by many writers, particularly in the last decade. Theoretically this therapy is based on the work of learning theorists. "The recent emergence of behavior therapy has been an implementation of learning theory based on didactic or interventionist approach" (42, p. 160). Skinner, Dollard and Miller, Murray and Mowrer are mentioned most often; Mowrer is generally cited for his two-factor learning theory model. As there has been no single learning theory, there likewise has been no single theory of behavioral therapy. There are, however, many common points among the behavioral writers. This chapter has been constructed with these common points in mind, in hopes that a general behavioral therapeutic system might grow out of these divergent views. As Kanfer has stated,

> The progress toward broader applications of learning principles in psychotherapy and toward construction of a technology of behavior therapy has been seriously impeded by the failure to combine interview and conditioning techniques (20, p. 174).

Bringing together divergent trainings is difficult. Klein, Dittman, and Parloff remark, "Despite their [behavioral counselors'] present enthusiasm for behavior therapy the fact remains that previously acquired skills still form an integral part of their repertoire (22, p. 265). Along with this relatively pessimistic note, come a few optimistic simplifications. "To oversimplify, the revolution [behavioral counseling] has overthrown 'um-hmm' and 'you-feel' replacing them with 'that's good' and 'try this' " (28, p. 81).

> Behavioral counseling is, thus far, restricted essentially to verbal conditioning. The counselor, to do behavioral counseling, needs only to be able to recognize types or classes of response and behavior made by the client, and to control his own responses so that he gives reinforcement solely for the types of client responses that are to be reinforced (47, p. 360).

Whether viewed with a jaundiced eye or in a euphoric state, behavioral therapy deserves the attention of the therapeutic community. Woody (48) has stressed its use for school counselors. Weitz has written about the application of techniques to produce new patterns of responses (43, p. 4), and Lazarus (27) has described its theoretical advantages. Only time and the test of therapeutic practice and research will uncover the real strengths or weaknesses of behavioral therapy.

SELECTED RESEARCH

Klein, et. al. attempted to improve the performance of underachievers through group counseling which stressed achievement skills in game playing and high achievement motivation learning (21). Sixty seventh- and eighth-grade students were divided randomly into the following four groups: training in achievement motivation, training in moderate risk taking, a combination of training in both achievement motivation and risk taking, and a control group. Results indicated no significant improvement in academic performances, and intercorrelations indicated no significant differences on the specific variables for which each group was trained. The authors concluded that variables under study and indicated by previous research did not significantly explain previous improvement of academic performance of underachievers. Many of the low achievers were not extreme risk takers nor apparently low in achievement motivation, as hypothesized from previous research. Furthermore, subjects who were in the achievement training group took more extreme risks while not increasing their test anxiety, thus raising questions as to whether risk taking, achievement, and test anxiety are necessarily related and integral with underachievers in general. Since all subjects selected as underachievers, then, were not as hypothesized, failure to find significant changes in academic improvement was perhaps to be expected due to these factors rather than to the precise method of counseling itself.

Using information from an earlier study, Thoresen and Krumboltz analyzed client information-seeking behavior outside of counseling as it related to counselor interview responses (41). One hundred ninety-two high school students were randomly assigned to counseling groups involving individual model reinforcement, group model reinforcement, individual reinforcement, group reinforcement, individual control film discussion, and a group control film discussion. Reinforcement counseling consisted of counselor verbal reinforcements to any client statement about information-seeking responses, while model reinforcement counseling used in addition a fifteen minute audio-taped model counseling interview presented at the beginning of the counseling session. Tapes analyzed eight verbal response categories believed to reflect the client-counselor interactions appropriate to the study. In addition to the tape analysis, external information-seeking behaviors for three weeks following the first counseling session were obtained by individual interviews with all 192 subjects and were analyzed for variety and frequency of occurrences of the observed behavior.

Results of the study indicated a positive low order relationship between counselor verbal reinforcement and corresponding information-seeking behavior outside the counseling session, positive correlations between counselor cue responses designed to elicit information-seeking responses and outside behavior, and a high correlation between counselor reinforcement of information-seeking responses and information-seeking by the client during the interview. In addition, model reinforcement subjects, even though viewing the film for part of the interview, on the average, had a significantly greater number of related outside behaviors than did the reinforcement only group. The authors concluded that counselors can apply the social learning paradigm to many educational, vocational, and personal problems through the design and use of specific procedures associated with client behavior occurring outside of the counseling session.

Hansen et al. compared the use of reinforcement counseling groups made up of all low sociometric students and model reinforcement counseling groups consisting of both high and low sociometric students to determine the efficacy of model reinforcement (17). The model group consisted of three boys and three girls with three students being high and three being low sociometric; it used models for both sexes. The reinforcement only group consisted of three high and three low and used no models. The control had no treatment, but consisted of both boys and girls, high and low. The groups met two times a week for four weeks and discussed specific weekly topics pertaining to social interaction and social maturity. Counselors reinforced statements and behaviors conducive to mature and acceptable social behavior. Model reinforcement groups improved sociometric status significantly more than either reinforcement alone or the control. Differential gain occurred with the model reinforcement group with respect to level of sociometric status (low gaining more), but there was no significant sex difference related to sociometric change. Students receiving reinforcement only made no significant improvement over the control group. No significant regression had occurred in a two-month follow-up survey.

Andrews reported on the successful use of behavior counseling in reducing excessive anxiety in underachievers (3). Two treatments were compared as to reduction in anxiety and raising achievement. Desensitization and reinforcement treatment was given for ten interviews to one treatment group of sixteen anxiety-displaying high school boys who had above average intelligence and below average achievement marks. Client-centered counseling was given to a similar group. Significant anxiety reduction occurred in the behavioral groups. However, hypotheses to the effect that behavior counseling would improve achievement were not supported. Andrews concludes

> Two important practical implications may be drawn from this experiment. First, the use of behavioral methods by regular school counselors is quite possible for them and need not be confined to the use of therapists with the highest level of training. Further, these approaches are altogether feasible within the school environment. Second, school counselors have few more pressing needs than their need for an effective method of assisting with the reduction in many students of excessive anxiety; this experiment indicates such a method (3, p. 96).

IMPLICATIONS FOR SCHOOL COUNSELORS

The theory of behavioral counseling lends itself to the school setting. It can be identified with the specificity demanded in so much school work and focuses on manageable factors or elements.

1. *Social sanction*—It has social sanction in its attention to school identified concerns, e.g., getting along with a teacher, improving one's study approaches.

2. *School press*—The institutional press permits behavioral counseling to select relevant factors. As noted in 1 above, the expectancies involved in the usual school press can be attended to in behavioral counseling.

3. *Counselor fit*—Some counselors would feel comfortable with the definitive nature of the goals of behavioral counseling.

4. *Counselor-pupil ratio*—The contemporary assignment of 400 or more students to counselors would not allow too much time for individualized counseling. Research evidence indicates that considerable counselor time is required for behavioral counseling.

5. *Counselor*—The counselor can define rather explicitly the concerns and motives to be considered. The businesslike approach and the delimited area of concern lends itself to trust in a particular

situation. Plan of action and counselor-counselee roles can be quite clearly identified.

6. *Counselee*—The counselee needs to reveal himself only in the limited area of behavior change. The specificity of focus on an element of behavior offers a pretty good chance for both counselor and counselee reward.

7. *Reality dimensions*—Time needed for behavior change will vary greatly. The nature of the behavior change is a key factor. For example, improvement of methods of seeking occupational information may take considerably less time than developing a better teacher-pupil relationship.

The reality key in behavioral counseling is whether the immediate reward will enhance long-term behavior change. Will the behavior change dissipate under the stress of the continuing conditions which served as a severe press on it in the first place? Will the conditioning ebb away when the reinforcers diminish in conscious awareness?

References

(1) American Psychological Association, *1969 Membership Register* (Washington, D.C., 1969).

(2) _____ *1970 Directory* (Washington, D.C., 1970).

(3) Andrews, W. R., "Behavioral and Client-Centered Counseling of High School Underachievers," *Journal of Counseling Psychology, 18:* 2 (1971), pp. 93–96.

(4) Arbuckle, Dugald S., "Kinds of Counseling: Meaningful or Meaningless," *Journal of Counseling Psychology, 14* (May, 1967), pp. 219–25.

(5) Bandura, Albert, "Psychotherapy as a Learning Process," in Gary E. Stollak, Bernard G. Guerney, Jr. and Meyer Rothbery (eds.), *Psychotherapy Research* (Chicago: Rand McNally & Company, 1966), pp. 96–114.

(6) _____ *Principles of Behavior Modification* (New York: Holt, Rinehart and Winston, Inc., 1969).

(7) Bijou, Sidney W., "Implications of Behavioral Science for Counseling and Guidance," in John D. Krumboltz (ed.), *Revolution in Counseling* (Boston: Houghton Mifflin Company, 1966), pp. 27–48.

(8) Breger, Louis and James L. McGaugh, "Critique and Reformulation of 'Learning-Theory' Approaches to Psychotherapy and Neurosis," *Psychological Bulletin, 43* (May, 1965), pp. 338–58.

(9) Carkhuff, Robert R. and Bernard G. Berenson, *Beyond Counseling and Therapy* (New York: Holt, Rinehart and Winston, Inc., 1967).

(10) Evans, Richard, *B. F. Skinner: The Man and His Ideas* (New York: E. P. Dutton & Co., Inc., 1968).

(11) Eysenck, Hans J. (ed.), *Behaviour Therapy and the Neuroses* (London: Pergamon Press, Inc., 1960).

(12) _____ "Learning Theory and Behavior Therapy," in H. J. Eysenck (ed.), *Behaviour Therapy and the Neuroses* (London: Pergamon Press, 1960), pp. 4–21.

(13) _____ "New Ways in Psychotherapy," *Psychology Today, 1* (June, 1967), pp. 39–47.

(14) Fletcher, Frank M., "Comments on Behavioral Counseling," *The Counseling Psychologist, 1:* 4 (1969), pp. 62–65.

(15) Goodstein, Leonard D., "Behavior Theoretical Views of Counseling," in B. Stefflre (ed.), *Theories of Counseling* (New York: McGraw-Hill Book Company, 1965), pp. 140–92.

(16) Hall, Mary Harrington, "An Interview with 'Mr. Behaviorist' B. F. Skinner," *Psychology Today, 1* (September, 1967), pp. 21–23, 68–71.

(17) Hansen, James C., Thomas M. Niland, and Leonard P. Zani, "Model Reinforcement in Group Counseling with Elementary School Children," *The Personnel and Guidance Journal, 47* (April, 1969), pp. 741–44.

(18) Hilgard, Ernest R. and Gordon H. Bower, *Theories of Learning,* 3rd ed. (New York: Appleton-Century-Crofts, 1966).

(19) Jones, Mary Cover, "A Laboratory Study of Fear: the Case of Peter," in H. J. Eysenck (ed.), *Behaviour Therapy and the Neuroses* (London: Pergamon Press, Inc., 1960), pp. 45–51.

(20) Kanfer, Frederick H., "Implications of Conditioning Techniques for Interview Therapy," *Journal of Counseling Psychology, 13* (Summer, 1966), pp. 171–77.

(21) Klein, J. P., J. J. Quarter, and R. M. Lazer, "Behavioral Counseling of Underachievers," *American Educational Research Journal, 6* (May, 1969), pp. 415–23.

(22) Klein, Majorie H., Allen T. Dittmann, and Morris B. Parloff, "Behavior Therapy: Observations and Reflections," *Journal of Consulting and Clinical Psychology, 33* (June, 1969), pp. 259–66.

(23) Krumboltz, John D., "Behavioral Counseling: Rationale and Research," *Personnel and Guidance Journal, 44* (December, 1965), pp. 383–87.

(24) _____ "Behavioral Goals for Counseling," *Journal of Counseling Psychology, 13* (Summer, 1966), pp. 153–59.

(25) _____ "Promoting Adaptive Behavior: New Answers to Familiar Questions," in J. D. Krumboltz (ed.), *Revolution in Counseling* (Boston: Houghton Mifflin Company, 1966), pp. 3–26.

(26) _____ (ed.), *Revolution in Counseling* (Boston: Houghton Mifflin Company, 1966).

(27) Lazarus, A. A., "New Methods in Psychotherapy: A Case Study," in H. J. Eysenck (ed.), *Behaviour Therapy and the Neuroses* (London: Pergamon Press, Inc., 1960), pp. 144–52.

(28) McDaniel, H. B., "Counseling Perspectives," in J. D. Krumboltz (ed.), *Revolution in Counseling* (Boston: Houghton Mifflin Company, 1966), pp. 79–93.

(29) Michael, Jack and Lee Myerson, "A Behavioral Approach to Counseling and Guidance," *Harvard Educational Review, 32* (Fall, 1962), pp. 382–401.

(30) Mowrer, O. Hobart, *Learning Theory and Behavior* (New York: John Wiley & Sons, Inc., 1960), pp. 212–52.

(31) Murray, Edward J., "The Empirical Emphasis in Psychotherapy: A Symposium. Learning Theory and Psychotherapy: Biotropic versus Sociotropic Approaches," *Journal of Counseling Psychology, 10* (Fall, 1963), pp. 250–55.

(32) Phillips, E. Lakin and Salah El-Batrawi, "Learning Theory and Psychotherapy: With Notes and Illustrative Cases," *Psychotherapy: Theory, Research, and Practice* (Fall, 1964), pp. 145–50.

(33) Schaefer, Halmuth H. and Patrick L. Martin, *Behavioral Therapy* (New York: McGraw-Hill Book Company, 1969).

(34) Shertzer, Bruce, and Shelley C. Stone, *Fundamentals of Counseling* (Boston: Houghton Mifflin Company, 1968).

(35) Shoben, Edward J., Jr., "Psychotherapy as a Problem in Learning Theory," in H. J. Eysenck (ed.), *Behaviour Therapy and the Neuroses* (London: Pergamon Press, Inc., 1960), pp. 52–78.

(36) _____ "Personal Worth in Education and Counseling," in J. D. Krumboltz (ed.), *Revolution in Counseling* (Boston: Houghton Mifflin Company, 1966), pp. 13–21.

(37) Skinner, B. F., *Science and Human Behavior* (New York: The Macmillan Company, 1953).

(38) _____ "Behaviorism at Fifty," in T. W. Wann (ed.), *Behaviorism and Phenomenology* (Chicago: University of Chicago Press, Phoenix Books, 1964), pp. 79–97.

(39) Thoresen, Carl E., "Behavioral Counseling: An Introduction," *School Counselor, 14* (September, 1966), pp. 13–21.

(40) _____ "The Counselor as an Applied Behavioral Scientist," *Personnel and Guidance Journal, 47* (May, 1969), pp. 841-48.

(41) Thoresen, Carl E. and John D. Krumboltz, "Relationship of Counselor Reinforcement of Selected Responses to External Behavior," *Journal of Counseling Psychology, 14* (1967), pp. 140–44.

(42) Truax, Charles B., "Some Implications of Behavior Therapy for Psychotherapy," *Journal of Counseling Psychology, 13* (Summer, 1966), pp. 160–70.

(43) Weitz, Henry, *Behavior Change Through Guidance* (New York: John Wiley & Sons, Inc., 1964).

(44) Wilson, G. T., Alma E. Hannon, and W. I. M. Evans, "Behavior Therapy and the Therapist-Patient Relationship," *Journal of Consulting and Clinical Psychology, 32* (April, 1968), pp. 103–9.

(45) Wolpe, Joseph, *Psychotherapy by Reciprocal Inhibition* (Stanford, Calif.: Stanford University Press, 1958).

(46) Wolpe, Joseph and A. A. Lazarus, *Behavior Therapy Techniques* (London: Pergamon Press, Inc., 1966).

(47) Woody, Robert H., "Preparation in Behavioral Counseling," *Counselor Education and Supervision, 7* (Summer, 1968), pp. 357–62.

(48) _____ "Reinforcement in School Counseling," *School Counselor, 15* (March, 1968), pp. 253–58.

(49) Wrenn, C. Gilbert, "Two Psychological Worlds: An Attempted Rapprochement," in J. D. Krumboltz (ed.), *Revolution in Counseling* (Boston: Houghton Mifflin Company, 1966) pp. 95–106.

7 Trait-Factor Counseling

INTRODUCTION

Trait-factor counseling was first called *vocational guidance,* then *vocational counseling,* and now has its present nomenclature (23, p. 90). E. G. Williamson notes, "In this theory it is assumed that one of man's characteristics is that he is an organized pattern of varied capacities which may be identified through . . . psychological tests" (23, p. 90). This "school" of counseling has also been called the "Minnesota point of view" because its primary purveyors have been from the University of Minnesota.

The trait-factor approach to counseling addresses itself to the idea that man spends the greater part of his time attempting to bring order and reason into the major decisions in life (5, p. 105). Williamson defines counseling in this context:

> Counseling has been defined as a face-to-face situation in which, by reason of training, skill or confidence vested in him by the other, one person helps the second person to face, perceive, clarify, solve, and resolve adjustment problems (30, p. 92).

The careful reader will have noted the similarity of this definition with previous definitions in client-centered and developmental counseling.

The Minnesota point of view is heavily committed to students and youth, primarily in the college setting, and focuses much attention on the dilemmas faced by each youth. These dilemmas are "(1) which purposes or life objectives to choose in a thoughtful manner;

(2) to be or not to be in quest of immediate satisfaction; and (3) to strive to become or not to become one's highest and best potentiality" (27, p. 176).* Williamson's views of the dilemma of youth and his assumptions concerning the "nature of human nature" (24, p. 193) probably best sum up the major assumptional bases for trait-factor counseling. His eight assumptions regarding personality, work, and society are (24, pp. 194–95):

1. "Each person is an organized, unique pattern of capabilities and potentialities." Capabilities are identifiable by objective tests statistically designed and validated. For most individuals their capabilities are stable at maturity.
2. "These capacities are differently correlated with different work tasks, so that different capacities are significantly involved in different tasks or behavior." The relationships between work performances, interest, and personality should be verified by research so that successful workers in different tasks may be statistically identified as a stable basis upon which to build models of comparison.
3. "The task of succeeding in school curricula may be studied by research designs comparable to those used by industrial psychologists for differentiating occupations." Different curricula may require different capacities or interests.
4. "The diagnosis . . . of potential should precede choice of or assignment to or placement in work tasks or in curricula."
5. "Diagnoses of capabilities and interests before instruction facilitate learning."
6. "There is some degree of homogeneity . . . within each occupational criterion group."
7. The best predictor of success in these fields is obtained by a battery of trait tests.
8. Each individual has capabilities and seeks to identify and utilize them.

Transparently, a heavy emphasis is placed on personality and interest assessments and other psychological devices. An equal emphasis is devoted to the use of external and objective criteria against

---

*Frank Parsons had similar views when he described the vocational guidance of youth: "(1) a clear understanding of yourself, your aptitudes, abilities, interests, ambitions, resources, limitations, and their causes; (2) a knowledge of the requirements and conditions of success, advantages, compensations, opportunities and prospects in different lines of work; (3) true reasoning on the relations of these two groups of facts" (8, p. 5).

which continuous research validation and refinement may be applied.

Credit for the trait-factor system has been laid upon the shoulders of various men. D. G. Paterson has cited the pioneer work of Frank Parsons (9, p. vii). On the other hand, C. H. Patterson has named Paterson for his studies of individual differences and test development (10, p. 17). Williamson on one occasion traces trait-factor vocational counseling to early German and French concepts of personality (24, p. 193), but in another work gives credit to Parsons, Harper, and Witmer (23, pp. 72–89). Parsons' work with early vocational planning and the Breadwinners' College has been known for many years (23, p. 76). The work of William Rainey Harper, the first president of the University of Chicago, has been ignored until rather recently. It was Harper who advocated the scientific study of the student, individualized education, faculty advising, and a whole host of services which today are part of college student personnel programs (23, pp. 81–86). Witmer is noted for his contributions via the psychological clinic (23, pp. 86–89).

Of all the writers concerned with trait-factor counseling, the most known is E. G. Williamson. Williamson's work has added substance, form, and order to this type of counseling. Williamson's major contributions have been: *Student Personnel Work: An Outline of Clinical Procedures,* 1937, with Darley (29); *How to Counsel Students: A Manual of Techniques for Clinical Counselors,* 1939 (14); *Counseling Adolescents,* 1950 (15); "Vocational Counseling: Trait-Factor Theory," 1965 (24); *Vocational Counseling: Some Historical, Philosophical and Theoretical Perspectives,* 1965 (23); and *The American Student's Freedom of Expression,* 1966, with Cowan (28).

BIOGRAPHICAL DATA

Edmund Griffith Williamson was born August 14, 1900. He earned his baccalaureate degree at the University of Illinois in 1925 and his doctorate from the University of Minnesota in 1931. As a graduate student at the University of Minnesota, Williamson worked under Donald G. Paterson. Paterson so influenced Williamson's life that he has never forgotten his early mentor. Nearly all his books speak of Paterson, and his latest theoretical offering is dedicated to Paterson, "pioneering innovator in adapting industrial research design and military classification techniques in the counseling of college student clientele" (23).

In 1932 Williamson became the first director of the University of Minnesota Testing Bureau. In 1939 he became coordinator of student personnel services at the same university. Since 1941 he has been dean of students at Minnesota, a position he still holds. Williamson is a diplomate in counseling psychology of the American Board of Examiners in Professional Psychology and a past president of the American Personnel and Guidance Association (1967).

PHILOSOPHY AND CONCEPTS

The trait-factor, or Minnesota, approach to counseling is related to education, particularly at the college and university level. The first chapter of *Counseling Adolescents* is titled "Counseling as Education" (15). *Student Personnel Work* has "American Education" as a first chapter (29). *How to Counsel Students: A Manual of Techniques for Clinical Counselors* starts with "The Role of Student Personnel in Education" (14). This view is even more closely related to education by the assertion that "the basic purpose of education is not only to train the intellect but also to assist students to achieve those levels of social, civic, and emotional maturity which are within the range of their potentialities" (15, p. 38). Further:

> Counseling is as fundamental a technique of assisting the individual to achieve a style of living satisfying to him and congruent with his status as a citizen in a democracy as are the instructional techniques used by the teacher . . . to achieve stipulated academic or educational goals (15, p. 3).

This emphasis has not changed throughout Williamson's writings; a key chapter in *Vocational Counseling* is "Discovering the Individual Student in Education" (23, ch. 4).

Shertzer and Stone claim: "Fundamental to trait and factor counseling is the assumption that man seeks to use self-understanding and knowledge of his abilities as a means of developing personality" (11, p. 247). And Williamson has noted:

> The foundation of modern concepts of counseling rests upon the assumption of the unique individuality of each child and also upon the identification of that uniqueness through objective measurement as contrasted with techniques of subjective estimation and appraisal (23, p. 56).

Carkhuff and Berenson identify a "strong deterministic base to the trait-and-factor approach" (5, p. 106), and Arbuckle notes this in much of Williamson's writings (2, p. 269).

> I am suggesting, of course, that the counselor has available techniques for helping the student to employ rational and cognitive efforts to control the nature and direction and rate of change in himself (20, p. 615).

> And most important of all presuppositions is the point that counselors should openly enter into the counseling relationship with a 'normative bias.' And our bias is the source of our eternal optimism that our students will aspire to the 'good' life of truth beauty, rationality, and 'full humanity' (26, p. 623).

Counseling itself has been referred to in various ways by the trait-factor counselors. Some of the definitions seem more like the eclectic counselor: "The counselor is ready to advise with the student as to a program of action consistent with, and growing out of, the diagnosis" (15, p. 233). Others have a client-centered ring: "Counseling . . . [is] a face-to-face situation in which . . . one person helps the second person to face, perceive, clarify, solve and resolve adjustment problems" (30, p. 192). There is even a touch of behaviorism in some definitions:

> But I feel certain that a counselor can play a significant role in helping the individual to perceive, and to accept emotionally, the inevitability of authority in some form or another acting as a restrictive agency upon the individual's free play of self-directed freedom (25, p. 213).

Williamson prefers the term *counseling,* as opposed to *guidance,* in referring to the relationship between counselor and client. Occasionally the term *interview* has been used and even *seminar:* "But in the continuing seminar, which we call counseling, the 'becoming opportunity' is one experience in which alternative value commitments are identified as available for choice" (27, p. 177). The word *client,* used in most therapies, is replaced by the term *individual* or, more commonly, *student* in trait-factor writings. This use of the word *student* is but another indication of the educational emphasis of this theory.

The role of the counselor in this system centers around diagnosis and information giving. Williamson comments, "In a very substantial way, counseling involves information giving and collecting, but it is information of a profound sort having to do with the development of a human being" (24, p. 200). "In a sense, the counselor brings external information to help the individual 'measure' himself" (24, p. 199). The general concepts of the trait-factor theory essentially deal with the counselor and the student.

CONCEPTION OF MAN

Williamson lists five basic questions concerning the nature and conception of man which counselors must answer. Indeed, these questions must not only be answered, but the answers must be continually evaluated and sharpened.

1. "What is the nature of human nature? What is the nature of man?" (23, p. 182). The counselor should believe that man is capable of learning to solve his problems. He must maintain an optimistic hopefulness. "Man is born with the potential for both good and evil and that the meaning of life is to seek good and reject—or at least control—evil" (23, p. 183). "Man is a rational being" (23, p. 201).

2. "What is the nature of human development?" (23, p. 183). There are widely divergent views concerning human development which may be best handled by an eclectic approach.

3. "What is the nature of the 'good life' and 'the good'?" (23, p. 185). Each counselee must think provisionally and tentatively about this concept. He must carry on his private intellectual search in his own seminar by continuously evaluating his provisional answers.

4. "What is the nature of the determination of the good life?" (23, p. 188). The problem here has been who would determine what is good. Counseling must aid students in determining the good life for themselves.

5. "What is the nature of the universe, and what is man's relationship to that universe?" (23, p. 189). The verve with which the counselor counsels "will be determined by his attitude of hopefulness and anticipation that man's efforts to become will be 'determinative' in the outcome of the human enterprise" (23, p. 189).

An additional assumption presented by Williamson concerns the "Value of the Human Enterprise" (23, p. 203). He states that the attainment of success and satisfaction is, at least in part, a function

of the similarity between an individual's talents and the requirements of the life for which he is striving, be it vocational, academic,
or personal.

RELATED THEORY OF PERSONALITY

As described by Williamson, the Minnesota School of Counseling
"embraces a theory of personality discussed under the rubric 'trait-
factors' (23, p. 90). In another work Williamson says, "The learning
theory underlying the trait-factor type of counseling embraces the
development of human personality from infancy to adulthood" (24,
p. 196). [It has been assumed that there is a developmental pattern
from infancy to adulthood (24, p. 196).] He continues, "A second
aspect of learning theory . . . concerns man's cognitive capacity as
applied to the task of controlling himself, profoundly and comprehensively" (24, p. 197).

To this information on personality theory and trait-factor counseling, Williamson adds seven assumptions which he traces from
their origin. These assumptions, carefully elaborated in his text, are
summarized here (23, pp. 204–5):

1. Human capabilities are unique in their individualized config-
   uration. Aptitudes and abilities are capable of being trained,
   at least partially, into people.
2. Aptitudes and abilities are psychometrically measurable.
3. It is possible to compare human characteristics when they
   are evaluated or measured in the same units.
4. Men and their vocational capabilities and aptitudes can be
   measured and standardized so as to establish occupational
   criterion groups. There is an age where men become more
   stable in these capacities and aptitudes.
5. Interests can also be measured and standardized, and reach
   a peak of stability.
6. Understanding of the personality maturation of a normal
   pattern is important to the counselor.
7. The necessity of therapy is to help students feel better, develop normally, and think clearly.

THEORY OF THERAPY

Like some of the other psychotherapeutic writers,
trait-factor counselors impose conditions on the counseling process.

Conditions precede process, which is implemented by techniques on the way toward goals. Williamson gives seventeen conditions, meant to be illustrative only, which are summarized as follows (23, pp. 205–14):

1. The purpose of counseling and the techniques employed by the counselor will help the student develop in all aspects of his personality.
2. There is a precious uniqueness to the individual human which comes into full development only within the context of relationship with others.
3. The counseling relationship need not be strictly voluntary to be mutually productive.
4. Counseling should not be entirely centered upon students who exhibit problems.
5. Counselors need to deal clearly with the concept of counselor influence in the interview. It is doubtful that complete neutrality is possible.
6. Counselors have a responsibility to society, either "macro" or "micro." The counselor must do more than exhibit unconditional acceptance.
7. The interdependence and totality of human growth and development must be considered in counseling.
8. The student must be understood to be progressing through a series of life stages of development.
9. The counselor must deal with the whole student, not become focused just on the parts.
10. The balance between man's thinking and feeling must be understood. Either may at times be distorted.
11. The concept of "insight" deserves reexamination. It may be overemphasized.
12. Counseling about self-development is not restricted to any group or class. It is open to everyone.
13. The reinforcements for a good life must be understood in the light of the breadth or narrowness of individuality and society.
14. Counseling, like education, must be organized around the idea that students develop their own potential and help others to develop at the same time.
15. Counselors need to help the student understand that development has a nonlinear curve. There are periods of acceleration, regression, and even changes to new directions.

16. Concepts of excellence may serve as guidelines for human striving.
17. Counselors must have a profound respect for what man has been, is, and may become.

PROCESS

Because the individual's freedom to become can include self-destructive and antisocial forms of individuality, the trait-factor counselor seeks openly and frankly to influence the direction of development (17, p. 3). Counselors of the Minnesota point of view do not advise waiting for students to seek help, but suggest devising subtle ways to get people in for help (17, p. 10).

According to Williamson, diagnosis is "the cooperative interpretation and identification of potentialities, as well as aspirations and motivations" (24, p. 200). In this sense, diagnosis takes the form of a series of hypotheses, based on conversation and psychometrics, which are tested by the student (24, p. 200). Bordin has said, "For Williamson, diagnosis is the effort to decide whether or not a person is operating on misinformation as he proceeds in his decision making" (4, p. 112).

The trait-factor counselor can influence students but should not determine the value commitments adopted by students (18). Williamson and Darley list six steps in the clinical process for trait-factor counselors (29, pp. 168–78)*:

1. "Analysis." The counselor must select those techniques which will best apply to the student. Tests, records, and experiences are all part of the data for analysis.
2. "Clinical synthesis." This is the orderly assembling of the extensive facts gathered in analysis.
3. "Clinical diagnosis." Diagnosis is aimed at describing the problems or problem complexes into one of six classifications: financial, educational, vocational, social-emotional-personal, family, health or physical-disability problems.
4. "Prognosis." The prognosis is the counselor's prediction concerning the student's use of alternative recommendations given to him.
5. "Treatment." Treatment is whatever is done by the institution, counselor, or student to enact the recommendations selected by the student.

---

*The same list appeared in Williamson's 1939 text *How to Counsel Students* (14) and in his 1950 text *Counseling Adolescents* (15), but in slightly different forms.

6. "Follow-up." Follow-up is the procedure of checking back on the case to see what happened. There are four purposes of follow-up: (1) to complete the clinical analysis; (2) to check on the treatment provided; (3) to see if any additional problem has arisen after the first diagnosis; (4) to evaluate the effectiveness of counseling.

TECHNIQUES

The most obvious technique used by trait-factor counselors is reliance on psychometry. Froehlich and Darley emphasize this, writing: "Tests should be used with supplementary techniques" (6, p. 3). The supplementary techniques referred to are interview techniques, which implies that tests are more important than interview data.

Techniques should be individualized for each student. As Williamson observes, "The counselor adopts his specific techniques to the individuality and problem pattern of the student, making the necessary modification to produce the desired result for a particular student" (15, p. 220). In one of Williamson's earlier books he lists five additional techniques for counseling (14, pp. 130–45):

1. "Establishing rapport." This is accomplished with the personal, concerned atmosphere the counselor creates with the student.
2. "Cultivating self-understanding." The counselor's attempts in this area are based upon his diagnosis and the student's own understanding.
3. "Advising." Advising must begin at the student level of understanding.* The counselor uses the student's own point of view, goals, and abilities as a basis of his advice. The three methods of advising are direct, persuasive, and explanatory (14, p. 139).
4. "Carrying out the plan." The counselor may help the student directly in carrying out the procedures arrived at in counseling.
5. "Referral." If the counselor is unable, or unwilling, to help the student carry out plans made, he should refer the student to the appropriately trained person or agency to implement the plan.

Williamson has mentioned another technique which is more subtle. "I believe that there are desirable characteristics of the coun-

---

*This point was handled in a different way in Williamson's 1950 text *Counseling Adolescents* (15), p. 233.

selor as a human being which may be intimately related with the effectiveness of counseling" (19, p. 109). The counselor himself thus becomes a potent technique in the counseling interview.

GOALS

The goals of trait-factor counseling are not so detailed as the conditions, processes, or techniques. Some of the goals as viewed by Williamson seem to be:

1. Counselors should be used by students for good purposes in seeking the good life (26, p. 617).
2. Counselors should "aid the individual in successive approximations of self-understanding and self-management . . ." (24, p. 190).
3. Counselors should help students "choose goals which will yield maximum satisfaction within the limits of those compromises necessitated by . . . society itself" (15, p. 221).

SUMMARY

The Minnesota school of counseling has had as its primary advocate E. G. Williamson. He has served the University of Minnesota in various capacities continuously since 1931. To be sure there have been other contributors to the theory: D. G. Paterson, J. G. Darley, C. P. Froehlich, and others. To these names Williamson would add D. E. Super, who "would probably classify himself along with Parsons as a trait-factor theorist" (24, p. 197). Nevertheless, the major theorizing has been done almost entirely by Williamson.

The trait-factor point of view relies heavily on psychometrics and prediction. In general the conditions of therapy are conditions for the counselor. The process consists mainly of gathering data, synthesizing it, forming a diagnosis, and planning a program for the student. The techniques used by the counselor revolve around establishing rapport, cultivating self-understanding, advising, and carrying out the advice. The goals have to do with self-understanding, choice of appropriate goals, and striving for the "good life." Williamson has become immersed in the informational aspects of decisions and the counselor's role in helping people make decisions (4, p. 112).

Some of Williamson's writing illustrates a definite deterministic approach: "Rather is counseling . . . value-oriented and not open-ended both regarding goals sought through aspirations and strivings of both counselor and student within their relationship" (16). Williamson is more direct than many counselors, probably because he has more faith in the counselor's ability to gather and analyze facts than he does in the student's. He has recognized the student's propensity to make irrational cognitive as well as emotional decisions. He has therefore taken a firmer hand in the interview so as not to reinforce the wrong behavior. "My point is that the psychotherapist's concept of permissiveness may indeed, prove to be too much freedom prerequisite to becoming one's full human potentiality" (27, p. 175).

In his more recent writings, Williamson has dealt with the affective aspects of counseling; nevertheless, the trait-factor approach remains essentially a rational, problem-solving approach. He has attempted to vary the diagnostic procedures with each individual, but this variance involves primarily a change in the psychometric schedule of the student rather than a different approach.

To study Williamson's position one must search diligently for ideas. The concepts of his theory are not found in one, two, or even three sources. His books are primary, but little cohesiveness of theoretical stance can be formulated without his journal contributions. Even his most recent summaries of the theory (1965) (24; 22) lack the order necessary for outlining.

Research is a strong emphasis of the theory. Williamson's most recent book is an excellent example of the detailed, well organized type of research that trait-factor theorists have done (28). Williamson places high value on psychological testing in the best tradition of the psychological laboratory. Much of the psychometric research done by Strong and Kuder has also been incorporated by the proponents of the Minnesota point of view. It is of particular importance to these theorists to establish common or normative behavior whether it be academic, vocational, or personal-social. This normative bias is essential to appropriate diagnosis. Williamson sums up this view when he writes:

> Let me make explicit my personal belief, or hypothesis, that the counseling relationship does add significantly to human development. But I also hypothesize that research, rather than tribal dogma, will be productive in establishing whatever that relationship does, in actuality, contribute to human development (21, p. 859).

SELECTED RESEARCH

In his book *Theories of Counseling* Buford Stefflre presents some of the earlier research evidence that indicates the widespread and continuing attempts to improve, refine, and revise this theory of counseling (13, pp. 207–12). He first sighted E. K. Strong Jr.'s follow-up study of the tested interest of seniors of Stanford University. Eighteen years later 85 percent of the former seniors were engaged in the occupation in which they received their highest ratings of measured interest. Stefflre also cited Stone's study which found that students in experimental groups tended to adjust their vocational choices to more appropriate levels than students in the control groups who did not receive vocational counseling and course instruction in vocational orientation. In addition, Stefflre presented a study by Gonyea which found that the past counseling ratings of appropriateness of choice were significantly more appropriate than precounseling objectives.

A more recent illustrative type of research concerning trait-factor theory of counseling is the Biggs, Roth, and Strong study concerned with identifying and measuring self-made academic predictions of entering college freshmen (3). The College Opinion Survey (COS) was constructed for this project. This survey consisted of sixteen items, of which eight were drawn from the General Self-Concept of Ability to Learn Scale (GSCOA) and eight from the Importance of Achieving Higher Grades than Others Scale (IG). Approximately 4300 entering freshmen in the College of Liberal Arts at the University of Minnesota were given the COS in the fall of 1968. Random samples of students were drawn from the 4300 freshmen. Past performance was measured by the student's percentile rank in his high school class at the end of his junior year. The student's grade point average at the conclusion of his first quarter at the University of Minnesota was used to measure future academic performance. The Minnesota Scholastic Test was used to measure the student's scholastic aptitude. The researchers concluded, "The results of this study show that self-made academic predictions based on students' estimates of how well they think they will perform relative to other students have strong relationships with past performance, scholastic aptitude, future performance, and interest in academic achievement" (3, pp. 84–85). The results also suggested that "self-made academic predictions are heavily influenced by the student's observations of his past performance relative to that of other students and by his projections of his relative ability position in possible competition groups."

Smith, Tseng, and Mink conducted a study to construct and validate a scale that could be easily administered and quickly scored for discriminating between those high school students who will drop out of school and those who will not (12). A scale containing thirty-four items was constructed and adjusted to a fifth grade level of reading. The scale was administered to 118 dropouts and 113 high school seniors with matching age and IQ. The results revealed a significant difference between the seniors and the dropouts in the following three classes: (1) pattern of failure or a failure syndrome; (2) involvement in extracurricular activities; (3) those factors that could best be described as home life or background. The dropouts had a greater distance to cover in going to school, but not enough to be significant.

Omvig investigated the effects of motivational guidance activities from the results of standardized achievement testing (7). The sample consisted of 135 students selected as an experimental group and 135 additional students selected for a control group. All the students were randomly selected from a midwestern community. Both groups were administered the Iowa Test of Educational Development, but only the experimental group was given help prior to testing. Short, individual conferences were arranged with each student in the experimental group. Also, the students of the experimental group attended a session to help orient them to taking tests. The findings revealed that the students in the control group had slightly higher mean scores on two of the five subtests; however, the students of the experimental group achieved higher scores on all subtests. Also, the students of the experimental group had scores that were significantly higher on the English and mathematics subtests.

IMPLICATIONS FOR SCHOOL COUNSELORS

1. *Social sanction*—Trait-factor approaches have social sanction by the very nature of limited coverage on socially acceptable items of behavior, e.g., learning arithmetic, interests in selected job areas.

2. *School press*—The press of the school objectives for learning is a powerful support for analyzing traits and learning experiences relating to them.

3. *Counselor fit*—The school counselor can feel comfortable with the specific analyses of traits and related factors to learning. His preparation seems to fit nicely into the testing and interpreting of traits and related learning experiences.

4. *Counselor-pupil ratio*—The analysis of traits and factors in learning lends itself to large numbers of students. Interpretation to groups, staff, and pupils is feasible.

5. *Counselor*—(a) Exploration of concerns: the trait-factor approach to counseling permits a fragmented approach with many voids. Generalizations are too easily given to fill in the many unknown traits and their interrelationships.

(b) Dependable motives: the trait-factor approach seems to rely on the quality of motivation of both counselor and pupil to perform. It neglects intervening variables of one's contemporary condition in life.

(c) Testing for trust: the trust is shifted from personal relationships to trust of instruments and their results.

(d) Planning for action: planning for action revolves around the expansion of specific trait-factor diagnoses into general plans of action. The trait-factor approach does give a specific basis for action.

(e) The school counselor participates in counseling largely through the process of interpretation as to the meaning of trait-factor analyses.

References

(1) American Psychological Association, *1970 Membership Register* (Washington, D.C., 1970).

(2) Arbuckle, Dugald S., *Counseling: Philosophy, Theory and Practice* (Boston: Allyn and Bacon, Inc., 1965).

(3) Biggs, Donald A., John D. Roth, and Stanley R. Strong, "Self-Made Academic Predictions and Academic Performance," *Measurement and Evaluation in Guidance, 3* (Summer, 1970), pp. 81–85.

(4) Bordin, Edward S., *Psychological Counseling,* 2nd ed., (New York: Appleton-Century-Crofts, 1968).

(5) Carkhuff, Robert R. and Bernard G. Berenson, *Beyond Therapy and Counseling* (New York: Holt, Rinehart and Winston, Inc., 1969).

(6) Froehlich, Clifford P. and John G. Darley, *Studying Students* (Chicago: Science Research Associates, Inc., 1952).

(7) Omvig, Clayton P., "Effects of Guidance on the Results of Standardized Achievement Testing," *Measurement and Evaluation in Guidance, 4* (April, 1971), pp. 47–52.

(8) Parsons, Frank, *Choosing a Vocation* (Boston: Houghton Mifflin Company, 1909).

(9) Paterson, Donald G., "Introduction," in E. G. Williamson and J. G. Darley (eds.), *Student Personnel Work* (New York: McGraw-Hill Book Company, 1937), pp. vii–xvi.

(10) Patterson, C. H., *Theories of Counseling and Psychotherapy* (New York: Harper & Row, Publishers, 1966).

(11) Shertzer, Bruce and Shelley C. Stone, *Fundamentals of Counseling* (Boston: Houghton Mifflin Company, 1968).

(12) Smith, John E., M. S. Tseng, and Oscar G. Mink, "Prediction of School Dropouts in Appalachia: Validation of a Dropout Scale," *Measurement and Evaluation in Guidance, 4* (April, 1971), pp. 31–37.

(13) Stefflre, Buford, *Theories of Counseling* (New York: McGraw-Hill Book Company, 1965).

(14) Williamson, E. G., *How to Counsel Students: A Manual of Techniques for Clinical Counselors* (New York: McGraw-Hill Book Company, 1939).

(15) _____ *Counseling Adolescents* (New York: McGraw-Hill Book Company, 1950).

(16) _____ "Value Orientation in Counseling," *Personnel and Guidance Journal, 36* (April, 1958), pp. 520–28.

(17) _____ "Some Issues Underlying Counseling Theory and Practice," in W. E. Dugan (ed.), *Counseling Points of View* (Minneapolis: University of Minnesota Press, 1959), pp. 1–13.

(18) _____ "Value Commitments and Counseling," *Teachers College Record, 62* (May, 1961), pp. 602–8.

(19) _____ "The Counselor as Technique," *Personnel and Guidance Journal, 41* (October, 1962), pp. 108–11.

(20) _____ "Counseling as Preparation for Directed Change," *Teachers College Record, 65* (April, 1964), pp. 613–22.

(21) _____ "An Historical Perspective of the Vocational Guidance Movement," *Personnel and Guidance Journal, 42* (May, 1964), pp. 854–59.

(22) _____ "The Place of Counseling Theory in College Programs," in B. Stefflre (ed.), *Theories of Counseling* (New York: McGraw-Hill Book Company, 1965), pp. 242–56.

(23) _____ *Vocational Counseling: Some Historical, Philosophical and Theoretical Perspectives* (New York: McGraw-Hill Book Company, 1965).

(24) _____ "Vocational Counseling: Trait-Factor Theory," in B. Stefflre (ed.), *Theories of Counseling* (New York: McGraw-Hill Book Company, 1965), pp. 193–214.

(25) _____ "The Fusion of Discipline and Counseling in the Educative Process," in B. N. Ard, Jr. (ed.), *Counseling and Psychotherapy* (Palo Alto, Calif.: Science and Behavior Books, Inc., 1966), pp. 208–16.

(26) _____ "Value Options and the Counseling Relationship," *Personnel and Guidance Journal, 64* (February, 1966), pp. 617–23.

(27) _____ "Youth's Dilemma: To Be or to Become," *Personnel and Guidance Journal, 46* (October, 1967), pp. 173–77.

(28) Williamson, E. G. and John L. Cowan, *The American Student's Freedom of Expression* (Minneapolis: University of Minnesota Press, 1966).

(29) Williamson, E. G. and J. G. Darley, *Student Personnel Work: An Outline of Clinical Procedures* (New York: McGraw-Hill Book Company, 1937).

(30) Williamson, E. G. and J. D. Foley, *Counseling and Discipline* (New York: McGraw-Hill Book Company, 1949).

8 Rational-Emotive Counseling

INTRODUCTION

Rational-emotive counseling or psychotherapy has much in common with other major schools of counseling and psychotherapy presented in this book. Developed by Albert Ellis, it incorporates many of the ideas of learning theory, psychoanalytic theory, and existential phenomenological theory, emphasizing the unique importance of cognitive, affective, and behavioral variables and their interrelationships to the counseling process. What differentiates rational-emotive theory from other approaches is the manner in which Ellis has integrated elements from rather diverse points of view into a meaningful theoretical framework and technique.

BIOGRAPHICAL INFORMATION

Dr. Albert Ellis, the founder of rational-emotive counseling and psychotherapy, was born in Pittsburgh, Pennsylvania and received his Ph.D. degree in clinical psychology from Columbia University. He has served on the faculties of Rutgers University and New York University and has had extensive involvement with various mental health agencies. He is currently the executive director

This chapter was especially prepared for this book by Donald J. Tosi, Ph.D., The Ohio State University.

of the Institute for Rational Living in New York City, where he is in private practice.

Albert Ellis has authored and co-authored over a dozen books and more than 200 articles in various psychological, sociological, and psychiatric journals. Among his books are: *Reason and Emotion in Psychotherapy,* 1962 (9); *How to Live with a Neurotic,* 1957 (11); *Creative Marriage,* with Robert A. Harper, 1961 (12); *A Guide to Rational Living,* with Robert A. Harper, 1961 (13); *The Art and Science of Love,* 1960 (8); and *Sex Without Guilt,* 1958 (10).

PHILOSOPHY AND CONCEPTS

Most discussions of the philosophical assumptions underlying counseling theories involve questions regarding the nature of man. For example, is man basically or intrinsically good, or is he evil? If he is basically evil, does he have the potential for good or vice versa? Other questions pertain to man's freedom. Is man free to initiate actions and choose between alternatives? Or is every human act predestined in the sense that it is impulsive or controlled largely by external factors?

In recent years, certain existential philosophers, such as Kierkegaard (17) and Heidegger (15), have taken the position that man by virtue of his existence is intrinsically good or worthwhile regardless of his achievements and the external evaluations ascribed to him by others. This view has become an integral part of the contemporary humanistic psychologies of Abraham Maslow (20), Carl Rogers (24), and Rollo May (21). The assumption that man is by nature good, rational, and forward looking opposes the early Freudian view that depicts man as hedonistic, selfish, and dominated by tensions emerging from conflicts between the id, ego, and superego.

While considerations of human worth or worthlessness may occupy a central position in many schools of psychotherapy and counseling, they are not necessarily basic to rational-emotive theory. These concepts, according to Ellis (9), are confusing because any reasonable notions about human worth that a person may determine for himself are contradicted by biological and social factors. Ellis suggests that while he cannot prove that a client is basically worthwhile because the client merely exists, the client cannot prove that he is basically worthless because he has not succeeded in life. Beliefs in personal worth or worthlessness have no empirical base and cannot be scientifically verified. If human worth has any meaning whatsoever to a person, it must be personal and experiential. According to Ellis:

> If personal value or worth is to have any tangible meaning—and quite possibly there is no very tangible meaning, apart from the vague definition that it can have—it would be better to relate it to one's own being and becoming (that is, one's becoming what one thinks or guesses one would like to become) than to the arbitrary, external notions of value that most of us unthinkingly connect it with (9, p. 158).

In most instances, a person will lead a more effective life if he believes and acts upon the assumption that life is worth living and realizes that he is the instrument of making life worthwhile through his own actions. If, on the other hand, a person believes that he is hopelessly inadequate, worthless, and incompetent, he will probably become depressed and unhappy. The Ellisonian position holds that man is capable of thinking and behaving in both rational and irrational ways. When man thinks rationally, he increases the probability of leading a more effective and happy life than when he thinks irrationally.

While dismissing as irrelevant most questions pertaining to man's essential nature, Ellis does believe that certain biological predispositions make it difficult for a person to be rational. Man seems to possess a biological proclivity to be psychologically disturbed and to become more disturbed as he interacts with his environment. For instance, man has a fundamental tendency to seek immediate gratification of his primary physiological needs (hunger, thirst, pain avoidance, and elimination). This biological predisposition also pervades psychological need states (achievement, order, affiliation, etc.) and is usually, although not always, modified through the process of socialization. The child, early in the developmental sequence, learns from parents and other significant role models and reinforcing agents that in order to get along in the world he must temporarily postpone the immediate gratification of certain physiological and psychological needs until a later and more appropriate time. That is, the child learns to discriminate, in accordance with situational requirements, between those need-based actions that are in his best interest and those which are not. This process (temporal integration), according to Ellis, is a prerequisite to later rational modes of thinking and acting. For instance, if a person desires an expensive automobile, but does not possess the financial

means to make the purchase, he does not have to become emotionally upset because his need was not gratified upon demand, even
though there is a natural tendency for him to be somewhat upset.
Nor does he have to become a nuisance to others. He can calmly
settle for a less expensive automobile in the short run. In the long
run, he may save his money, get a better job, and purchase the
expensive automobile.

If, however, a child is exposed to parental or other significant
role models who indoctrinate him with irrational ways of thinking
and behaving and reinforce him accordingly, he is quite likely to
display irrational modes of thinking and behaving later in life.
Again in the example of the expensive automobile, a person may
have a great desire to purchase the high-priced automobile regardless of the fact that he cannot afford it. If he purchases the automobile, he will obviously experience great pleasure in the short run. In
the long run, however, he may become terribly upset because he does
not have enough money to purchase other material things that he
strongly desires. Ellis lists several irrational beliefs or ideas that are
learned, for the most part, early in a person's life (9).

1. "The idea that it is a dire necessity for an adult human being
   to be loved or approved by virtually every significant other
   person in his community."
2. "The idea that one should be thoroughly competent, adequate, and achieving in all possible respects if one is to
   consider oneself worthwhile."
3. "The idea that certain people are bad, wicked, or villainous
   and that they should be severely blamed and punished for
   their villainy."
4. "The idea that it is awful and catastrophic when things are
   not the way one would very much like them to be."
5. "The idea that human unhappiness is externally caused and
   that people have little or no ability to control their sorrows
   and disturbances."
6. "The idea that if something is or may be dangerous or fear-
   some one should be terribly concerned about it and should
   keep dwelling on the possibility of its occurring."
7. "The idea that it is easier to avoid than to face certain life
   difficulties and self-responsibilities."
8. "The idea that one should be dependent on others and needs
   someone stronger than oneself on whom to rely."
9. "The idea that one's past history is an all-important deter-
   miner of one's present behavior and that because something

once strongly affected one's life, it should indefinitely have a similar effect."

10. "The idea that one should become quite upset over other people's problems and disturbances."

11. "The idea that there is invariably a right, precise, and perfect solution to human problems and that it is catastrophic if this perfect solution is not found."

The internalization and unquestioned adherence to any of these irrational ideas or beliefs constitutes the basis of most emotional disturbances.

Essentially, Ellis holds that emotional disturbances are the result of illogical or irrational thinking which occurs in the form of internalized sentences or verbal symbols that comprise an irrational system of beliefs. That is, emotional disturbances arise to a large degree from cognitive or thinking processes. He recognizes, however, that emotion is a complex mode of behavior which is integrally related to other sensing and response processes and states:

> Emotion, then, has no single cause or result, but can be said to have three main origins and pathways: (a) through sensori-motor processes (b) through biophysical stimulation mediated through the tissues of the autonomic nervous system and the hypothalmus and other subcortical centers and (c) through the cognitive or thinking processes. We may also, if we wish, add a fourth pathway and say that emotion may arise through the experiencing and recirculating of previous emotional processes (as when recollection of past feeling of anger triggers off a renewed surge of hostility) (9, p. 39).

Moreover, he also asserts:

> Among human adults reared in a social culture which includes a well-formulated language, thinking and emoting usually accompany each other, act in a circular cause and effect relationship, and in certain (though hardly all) respects are essentially the same thing. One's thinking often becomes one's emotion: and emoting under some circumstances becomes one's thought (9, p. 48).

The rational-emotive viewpoint emphasizes cognitive control over affective or emotional states. More specifically, one of the most direct ways of changing negative states, such as hostility, depression, or anxiety in human beings, is by altering those irrational beliefs and self-verbalizations which control such states. A person's internal verbalizations often occur at an unconscious or unaware level, and his negative affective states or emotional disturbances are not apparently associated with their spoken verbalizations. Thus, the counselor or therapist must accurately reveal to his clients their entire range of internal and external verbalizations and then vigorously challenge and attack these verbalizations (9, p. 339).

In summary, irrational thinking, which consists of internalized sentences or belief systems, originates early in the socialization process. Children can be literally indoctrinated with irrational ideas or beliefs by parents and significant others. While the child's thinking, emoting, and behaving may be initially under the control of others as he develops, these psychological and behavioral states come largely under his own control. Irrational thinking is associated with pernicious or self-defeating emotional states, such as excessive guilt, hostility, and anger, as well as their behavior manifestations.

THEORY OF COUNSELING

Rational-emotive counseling or psychotherapy is an active-directive, didactic approach. The counselor forcefully confronts the client with those irrational beliefs which are at the root of his disturbance and teaches him more rational ways of thinking and behaving. The goals of rational-emotive counseling are clearly both attitudinal and behavioral. That is, if the probability of successful counseling is to be maximized, the counselor must help the client reconstruct his thinking and belief system and also encourage him to engage in behavioral exercises that maximize positive environmental consequences.

Rational-emotive counselors employ most, if not all, of the proven counseling interventions developed by different schools of counseling and psychotherapy. Two major intervention techniques, however, are usually identified with the Ellisonian position. These are the application of the ABC theory of emotional disturbance and problem analysis and the systematic use of homework assignments.

Ellis's ABC principle of emotional disturbance emphasizes the importance of cognitive control over emotional states and their motivational counterparts. Ellis states:

This principle, which I have inducted from many psychotherapeutic sessions with scores of patients during the last several
years, was originally stated by the ancient Stoic philosophers,
especially Zeno of Citium (the founder of the School of Stoicism).
The truths of Stoicism were perhaps best set forth by Epictetus,
who in the first century A.D. wrote in The Enchiridion: 'Men are
disturbed not by things, but by the views which they take of
them.' Shakespeare, many centuries later, rephrased this
thought in Hamlet: 'There's nothing either good or bad but
thinking makes it so' (9, p. 54).

Ellis's ABC principle is consistent with phenomenological and
existential positions which emphasize the perceptual determinants
of behavior. The *A* represents a stimulus event external to the person; the *B* is generally the individual's attitude, beliefs, or interpretation of *A* in the form of verbal symbols or sentences; and *C* is the
person's reaction or response. *A* (the external stimulus) is not the
cause of *C* (the reaction or response); the cause of *C* is *B*. For example, a school counselor might explain to a client who blames a
teacher for upsetting him that it is not the teacher *(A)* who is the
source of the negative feeling *(C)*, but his own evaluation and interpretation of the teacher's behavior *(B)* that is responsible for his
negative reaction.

Typically, in an initial rational-emotive counseling interview
the counselor reduces most of the client's uncertainties about the
counseling process. He explains rather specifically the basic principles of rational-emotive counseling to the client and clearly delin-
eates their mutual responsibilities. The counselor clearly
communicates to his client that the counseling process is a learning
experience during which a person has an opportunity to examine
closely his ways of thinking and behaving. The client also learns that
he will be expected to implement and practice in outside situations
the new insights and learnings acquired during the counseling sessions. That is, the client must do his homework.

The major portion of the initial interview consists of the counselor's attempt to help the client articulate his concerns. The counselor must listen attentively to the client's verbalizations and may
resort to techniques such as reflection and clarification in his attempt to understand the client thoroughly and build a working relationship. The counselor and client cooperatively analyze the client's
problem situations and then decide upon appropriate behavioral
modification techniques. Since most clients will verbalize some degree of irrational thought during an initial session, the counselor
confronts the client at once with the ABC method of thinking and

problem analysis. Usually a homework assignment is given which may consist of having the client apply the ABC method to those outside situations in which he becomes emotionally upset. The client may also be required to read certain materials that illustrate rational ways of thinking and behaving. One book that serves this purpose is *A Guide to Rational Living* (Ellis and Harper) (13).

The rational-emotive counselor realizes the importance of establishing a sound relationship with his client. In many instances the client must be approached by the counselor in a warm, supportive, and permissive manner. The client should be helped to express himself freely. The rational-emotive counselor, however, does not believe that these relationship-building and expressive-emotive methods are likely to have much to do with getting to the core of the client's illogical thinking and induce him to think more rationally (9, p. 95).

Throughout the counseling process, the client is directly assisted by the counselor in recognizing and altering the internalized beliefs or ways of thinking which maintain his self-defeating emotional states and behaviors. To accomplish this, the counselor makes intensive use of the ABC method of problem analysis and confrontation.

During the initial stages of counseling, the active-directive confrontations of the rational-emotive counselor are sometimes met by client resistance (that is, the client attempts to perpetuate and defend his irrational ideas and behavior). The counselor directly and forcefully confronts the irrational elements of the client's resistance, even though he recognizes that working through some resistances may take several sessions. On this point, Ellis states:

> I also find, in the course of rational-emotive encounters, that persistent activity by the therapist often pays off. This is again to be expected on theoretical grounds, since if an individual's disturbances largely consist of the irrational sentences he has originally been indoctrinated with in his childhood and that he has kept telling himself ever since that time, it is only to be expected that such persistently ingrained indoctrinations will require a considerable amount of, shall we say, persistent "outgraining." This seems to be true of most learned habits: once they are distinctly overlearned, then, even though they lead to unfortunate results, it is difficult to unlearn them and to learn different habits; and the habituated individual must usually persist and persist in the unlearning and relearning process (9, p. 199).

The rational-emotive counselor, however, is careful not to overwhelm the client with the use of the ABC method. While the counselor's confrontations during the initial stages of counseling may focus upon the periphery of the client's problems, the counselor gets to the core of the client's disturbance as soon as possible.

The rational-emotive counselor is careful that he does not unwittingly reinforce the client's irrational thinking and behavior during and outside the sessions. Essentially, he punishes the client's irrational thinking, not in a vicious, hostile sense, but in a very objective and well-intentioned manner. When the client manifests reasonable modes of thinking and behaving, the counselor makes extensive use of positive social reinforcement. On this point Ellis states, "With this kind of highly active-directive, unpampering approach, I often find that I can push negativistic and inert people into self-healing action when a passive, non-directive technique would merely encourage them to continue their defeatist and defeating tendencies forever" (9, p. 198).

The systematic and deliberate use of confrontative techniques by the counselor, while necessary, is by no means sufficient. It is essential that the counselor help the client reconstruct those philosophic beliefs which control his self-defeating emotions. The counselor actively encourages the client to think in problem-solving terms. The counselor encourages the client (a) to generate alternative ways of thinking and acting, (b) to examine these alternatives in terms of their feasibility, and (c) to submit his new ideas to empirical test. More specifically, the counselor teaches the client to rethink, challenge, contradict, and reverbalize his internalized self-verbalization or beliefs so that his internalized beliefs become more logical and efficient.

Counseling from the rational-emotive viewpoint is a very demanding process because of the intense involvement of both the counselor and the client. The initial stages of rational-emotive counseling generally involve a great deal of counselor responsibility, but as the process continues, greater responsibility is assumed by the client.

To maximize the probability of successful outcomes and to expedite the counseling process, the counselor incorporates the use of homework assignments or behavioral tasks. The counselor's systematic use of homework assignments is an essential component of the counseling process. It is that component which permits the client to apply conscientiously to the outside world those behavioral modifying techniques discovered during the counseling encounters. Learning conditions are carefully and deliberately arranged by the counselor so that new patterns of thinking and behaving acquired by the client are transferred beyond the specific counseling situation.

Homework assignments usually consist of mnemonic exercises, such as the client applying the ABC method to those situational events or conditions under which he experiences negative emotional states (anxiety, guilt, depression) in combination with various assertive behaviors. In general, homework assignments are structured so that they successfully approximate the desired behavior, although there may be exceptions. Exposing a client to a highly threatening situation which he has not learned to cope with may simply generate avoidance behavior which would temporarily reduce his anxiety and simply reinforce the irrational ideas or beliefs he holds regarding such situations. For example, a young male, because he was rejected by some female in the past, becomes highly anxious when he thinks of asking another girl for a date. This anxiety is reduced when he simply avoids the situation. The young man, through his self-talk, may then convince himself that he is worthless, inadequate, or not like the other boys. The price he pays for the temporary reduction in anxiety could very well be a needless state of depression. Thus, he is caught in a vicious cycle.

In dealing with the problem, the rational-emotive counselor would encourage the client merely to engage in light conversation with members of the opposite sex. Once this has been successfully accomplished, and the client has learned to approach girls without experiencing needless anxiety, he is encouraged to ask a girl for a date. While engaging in these behavioral processes, the client employs the ABC method of analyzing his emotional reactions. Concomitantly with homework assignments, the counselor teaches the client to discriminate between thinking and acting. He points out to the client that while a girl may reject his actual offer for a date, this is not necessarily a catastrophic situation in and of itself but the thought of being rejected and its projected catastrophic consequences serve as an anxiety-producing stimulus. The counselor simply shows the client (through the ABC method) how this sort of irrational thinking brings about the client's anxiety and how the reduction of the anxiety (by avoiding girls) simply reinforces the avoidance behavior. Furthermore, the client is shown how he then, through his self-talk, proceeds to become depressed by labeling himself as worthless, no good, or inadequate. It is precisely this kind of client irrationality that is challenged and confronted by the rational-emotive counselor.

The purpose of homework is to help the client effect positive changes in his environment. By engaging in more appropriate behavior, the client is more likely to maximize positive and rewarding environmental consequences. Moreover, the client becomes less dependent upon the extrinsic reinforcements or incentives from the counselor and others. The client learns to substitute new thoughts or symbols that are associated with positive evaluations of his new accomplishments for his previous irrational ones. Such processes constitute the basis of positive self-reinforcement for one's own behavior.

As the counseling process evolves, the counselor's use of these techniques—the ABC method and homework assignments—becomes so inextricably interwoven that separating their unique contributions to the counseling process is rather difficult. Despite this difficulty, researchers have examined many of the procedures employed by rational-emotive counselors, singly and, in some cases, in combination with one another. Research in support of Ellis's theory has been provided by researchers of diverse theoretical orientations.

SELECTED RESEARCH

Research support for the rational-emotive counseling theory and techniques is based upon numerous investigations conducted in both laboratory and naturalistic settings. The research focuses upon four major areas: (1) The ABC theory of emotional disturbances (cognitive control over affective state); (2) use of extra-counseling assignments (homework); (3) efficacy of active-directive counseling intervention; and (4) comparisons of rational-emotive counseling with other approaches.

Studies which give credence to the ABC theory of emotional disturbance generally support the position that the interpretations which people place upon events determine their affective or emotional responses [Burkhead (4); Carlson, Travers, and Schwab (5); Schachter and Singer (25); Valens (31); Velton (32)]. In a laboratory investigation Carlson, Travers, and Schwab found that emotional responses (measured by Galvanic Skin Response) that were induced by electric shock could be modified when the subject's beliefs or expectations about the probability of being shocked were manipulated; that is, the greater the stated probability of being shocked, the more intense was the subject's emotional arousal (5). In a similar study, Velton found that when subjects read elation and depression statements, they would show the corresponding mood states (32).

More recently, Burkhead, in another laboratory investigation, found that a therapist using rational-emotive techniques could successfully reduce anxiety in subjects by manipulating their belief system (4). Burkhead employed both the GSR and the Multiple Affective Adjective Check List as measures of anxiety. Several case studies and investigations demonstrate the efficacy of extending treatment procedures beyond the specific counseling situation to the context in which the client's problem exists [Ayllon and Azrin (2); Walton and Mather (33); Garvey and Hegrenes (14); Kennedy (16)]. For example, Walton and Mather were able to reduce a client's phobia about people by having the client gradually become involved with people in social situations (33). Their technique approximates counterconditioning procedures. Garvey and Hegrenes (14) and Kennedy (16) have successfully employed graded performance tasks (successive approximations of the desired behavior) to reduce anxiety associated with the phobias of school children.

A substantial body of research is accruing which provides support for active-directive counseling and psychotherapeutic interventions [Anderson (1); Berenson, Mitchell, and Moravic (3); Lennard and Bernstein (19); O'Leary (22); Truax, Fine, Moravic, and Mills (30)]. The research findings by Anderson (1) and Berenson et al. (3) support the hypothesis that highly functioning counselors and psychotherapists employ higher frequencies of constructive confrontations than low-functioning counselors and therapists. Clients of the high-functioning counselor groups evidenced deeper levels of self-exploration than clients of the low-functioning groups. Moreover, Truax et al. have reported that persuasive potency of counselor and therapist is related to greater client improvement (30). That is, counselors and therapists who are highly persuasive seem to obtain higher client improvement rates than those who are low on persuasive potency.

The literature is replete with investigations of behavioral modification procedures which also support active approaches to counseling and psychotherapy [Rimm and Mahoney (23); Krumboltz and Schroeder (18); Thoresen and Krumboltz (26); Tosi, Upshaw, Lande, and Waldron (28); Tosi, Briggs, and Morley (27)]. These studies employed learning theory-derived interventions such as social modeling, social reinforcement, and desensitization procedures. For instance, Tosi, Upshaw, Lande, and Waldron found that verbal output of reticent elementary school children in a classroom situation could be increased by the counselor's active and systematic use of social reinforcement techniques (28).

Research which compares rational-emotive counseling to other approaches at the present time is limited. Research of this nature, however, is accruing. DiLoreto found that rational-emotive therapy was more effective than client-centered or learning-theory oriented approaches in reducing interpersonal anxiety of introverted clients (6). (The study was conducted in a university setting on a group counseling modality.) Dolgan examined the differential effects of desensitization procedures and rational-emotive therapy upon phobic behavior (7). Phobic subjects treated with rational-emotive therapy were judged to exhibit greater reductions in fear than subjects exposed to desensitization therapy. Another study which tested the effects of short-term social reinforcement and rational-emotive counseling on discipline problem students was conducted by Tosi, Vanderhill, Hanel, and Bolinger in a midwestern inner-city high school (29). In addition to the two counseling approaches, a non-counseling discussion group and an inactive control group were employed. While the mean difference in disciplinary office referrals between the four groups was not statistically significant, the findings were in the predicted direction. Subjects in the social reinforcement and rational-emotive counseling treatments showed a greater reduction in office referrals than subjects in the other two conditions. However, reductions in disciplinary office referrals did slightly favor social reinforcement counseling.

IMPLICATIONS FOR SCHOOL COUNSELORS

Rational-emotive theory and technique have rather profound implications for school counseling practice. However, in the final analysis, the effectiveness of this approach rests heavily on the compentency and skill of the counselor. The school counselor who practices rational-emotive counseling needs to possess high levels of skill and competency in interpersonal relationships, human growth and development, persuasiveness, and behavioral and attitudinal modifying procedures. Most importantly, the counselor must himself be rational or, to use a current term, "together," if he expects to provide his clients with a healthy model —the manifestation of that which rational-emotive theory embodies.

The notion is a simple one—a counselor will not help a client grow beyond the level to which the counselor himself has grown.

The rational-emotive model provides the school counselor with (a) a broad theoretical framework which assists him in conceptualizing and understanding many concerns of his client; (b) clinical and research-based interventions with which he can directly help clients to overcome their difficulties; and (c) most importantly, the means by which he helps clients sustain new ways of thinking and behaving. Rational-emotive counseling, in the form described in this chapter and with some modification, is extremely applicable to the school setting (grades K-12). Modifications of rational-emotive procedures are usually in accordance with the various psycho-social stages of human development. For instance, it may be extremely difficult for a counselor to communicate the ABC method of problem analysis to a first grade student and have that student immediately internalize each component in a meaningful way. This does not mean that the counselor cannot introduce his first grade client to the rudiments of rational thinking or other behavioral modifying procedures since the client is probably being indoctrinated with the antithesis of rational thinking elsewhere. The counselor may have to use his own creativity and ingenuity in such situations.

It is well-known that many aspects of the school situation are perceived and evaluated by most students in rather negative terms. While a student's assessment of a particular aspect of school may be quite accurate, his personal reactions to it may not necessarily be the most rational or appropriate. For instance, in response to a hostile or maladjusted teacher, a student may become needlessly and indiscriminately hostile, aggressive, depressed, or angry. Furthermore, these reactions may meet with negative consequences from parents, administrators, and teachers. Students who become involved in rational-emotive counseling normally acquire the philosophy that "it is wise to accept unpleasant people and circumstances when (a) it is of practical advantage to do so, or (b) there really is no choice" (9, p. 362). The student, for example, would be encouraged to accept this unfair or hostile teacher since it is quite likely that the teacher in question, despite his personal maladjustment, could have much to offer the student in terms of subject matter. The student may not be acting in his best interest if he confuses the teacher's personal problems with his academic expertise. This does not mean that the purpose of rational-emotive counseling is to adjust a person to his particular environment. On the contrary, the notion is simply that "a rational individual will strive to accept unpleasant conditions only temporarily and will do everything in his power (in spite of what others may think of him personally) to change these conditions" (9, p. 362).

In recent years, the peer group has emerged as a cultural modality in which youth find refuge from the world of parents, teachers, and other adult groups and institutions. For most youth, the peer group provides a base for psychological support and significant learning about human relationships. The peer group, however, may also provide conditions under which many new irrational modes of thinking and behaving are acquired. Oftentimes, it is the school counselor who has the task of assisting the student in making sense out of the peer group phenomenon. For instance, it is generally well known that some adolescent groups engage in and perpetuate a variety of practices, some of which involve sex and the excessive use of alcohol and drugs. A teenager, because of a strong desire for approval and acceptance by members of a group, may accept those group-approved practices or norms. Although the teenager is successful in immediately gratifying one need, he may be setting the stage for even greater problems in the future. He now risks the consequences of venereal disease and/or drug addiction. Moreover, he may get a girl pregnant and become a teenage husband who ends up in some sociological treatise on teenage divorce rates. For his actions, there is usually the associated high cost of guilt, shame, anxiety, or depression.

Rational-emotive counseling can be extremely valuable in helping a teenager overcome self-induced pressures in response to his environment—the family, the school, the peers, etc. The teenager can learn that he does not need complete and total acceptance from his peers or, for that matter, any other group or person. According to Ellis, the truly rational person

> will always be something of a rebel since only by rebelling against stultifying conformity to some degree can a human being in our society maintain a good measure of his own individuality. But he will not childishly rebel for the sake of rebelling. He will fight against unnecessary restrictions and impositions, temporarily accept what is truly inevitable and remain undisturbed whether he is fighting or accepting (9, p. 363).

Moreover, the rational-emotive counselor would assist the teenager to deal effectively with those negative and self-defeating emotions such as guilt and shame (self-blame) which often follow irrational actions. More specifically, the client is taught not to confuse objective acceptance of wrongdoing (my performance is poor because I made a mistake or behaved wrongly—now what do I do to become a more effective person) with pernicious self-blame (I am totally worthless because my behavior is wrong or bad—there is nothing I can do or say—all is lost).

Admittedly, only the surface has been touched in this discussion of the implications of rational-emotive theory for school counseling practices. The scope of this book precludes a detailed presentation on this topic. There is, however, an additional word or two for the practicing school counselor. In general, counselors are working toward similar ends in that they are trying to help their clients internalize a sensible philosophy of life. At times in our work, because we are fallible, we fail in our attempts to help some clients. When we do in spite of the fact of possible failure and the fact that we (rational-emotive counselors) refuse to define ourselves as hopelessly inadequate, worthless, and incompetent, we will persist in our efforts and derive much personal and professional satisfaction. After all, one can only do his best.

References

(1) Anderson, S. C., "Effects of Confrontation by High and Low Functioning Therapists," *Journal of Counseling Psychology, 15* (1968), pp. 411–16.

(2) Ayllon, T. and N. H. Azrin, "Reinforcement and Instructions with Mental Patients," *Journal of Experimental Analysis of Behavior, 7* (1964), pp. 327–31.

(3) Berenson, B. G., K. M. Mitchell, and J. A. Moravic, "Levels of Therapist Functioning, Patient Depth of Self-Exploration, and Type of Confrontation," *Journal of Counseling Psychology, 15* (1968), pp. 136–39.

(4) Burkhead, D. E., "The Reduction of Negative Affect in Human Subjects. A Laboratory Investigation of Rational-Emotive Psychotherapy," Ph.D. diss., Western Michigan University, 1970.

(5) Carlson, W. A., R. M. W. Travers, and E. A. Schwab, "A Laboratory Approach to the Cognitive Control of Anxiety," paper presented at the American Personnel and Guidance Association, April, 1969.

(6) DiLoreto, A., "A Comparison of the Relative Effectiveness of Systematic Desensitization, Rational-Emotive, and Client-Centered Group Psychotherapy in the Reduction of Interpersonal Anxiety in Introverts and Extroverts," Ph.D. diss., Michigan State University, 1969.

(7) Dolgan, J. J., "The Efficacy of Systematic Desensitization Procedures and a Rational Therapy in the Modification of Phobic Behavior," *Dissertation Abstracts, 28* (1968), 3774-B.

(8) Ellis, Albert, *The Art and Science of Love* (New York: Lyle Stuart, Inc., 1960).

(9) ———— *Reason and Emotion in Psychotherapy* (New York: Lyle Stuart, Inc., 1962).

(10) ———— *Sex without Guilt,* rev. ed. (New York: Lyle Stuart, Inc., 1966).

(11) ———— *How to Live with a Neurotic* (New York: Universal Publishing and Distributing Corporation, Award Books, 1969).

(12) Ellis, Albert and Robert A. Harper, *Creative Marriage* (New York: Lyle Stuart, Inc., 1961).

(13) ———— *A Guide to Rational Living* (Englewood Cliffs N.J.: Prentice-Hall, Inc., 1961).

(14) Garvey, W. P. and J. R. Hegrenes, "Desensitization Techniques in the Treatment of School Phobia," *American Journal of Orthopsychiatry, 36* (1966), pp. 147–52.

(15) Heidegger, Martin, *Being and Time,* J. Macquarrie and E. Robinson (trs.) (London: S. C. M. Press, 1962).

(16) Kennedy, W. A., "School Phobia: Rapid Treatment of Fifty Cases," *Journal of Abnormal Psychology, 70* (1965), pp. 285–89.

(17) Kierkegaard, Søren, *Philosophical Fragments,* D. F. Swenson (tr.) (Princeton, N.J.: Princeton University Press, 1962).

(18) Krumboltz, J. D. and W. W. Schroeder, "Promoting Career Planning through Reinforcement," *Personnel and Guidance Journal, 43* (September, 1965), pp. 19–25.

(19) Lennard, H. and A. Bernstein, *The Anatomy of Psychotherapy* (New York: Columbia University Press, 1960).

(20) Maslow, A. H., "Existential Psychology—What's in it for Us?" in R. May (ed.), *Existential Psychology* (New York, Random House, Inc., 1961), pp. 52–60.

(21) May, Rollo, "Contributions of Existential Psychotherapy," in R. May, E. Angel, and H. Ellenberger (eds.), *Existence: A New Dimension in Psychiatry and Psychology* (New York, Basic Books, Inc., Publishers, 1958), pp. 37–91.

(22) O'Leary, S. G., "Counselor Activity as a Predictor of Outcome," *Personnel and Guidance Journal, 48* (1969), pp. 135–39.

(23) Rimm, David C. and Michael J. Mahoney, "The Application of Reinforcement and Participant Modeling: Procedures in the Treatment of Snakephobic Behavior," *Behavioral Research and Therapy,* 7 (1969), pp. 369–76.

(24) Rogers, Carl R., *On Becoming a Person* (Boston: Houghton Mifflin Company, 1961).

(25) Schachter, S. and J. E. Singer, "Cognitive, Social, and Physiological Determinants of Emotional States," *Psychological Review, 69* (1962), pp. 379–99.

(26) Thoresen, C. E. and J. D. Krumboltz, "Similarity of Models and Clients in Behavioral Counseling: Two Experimental Studies," *Journal of Counseling Psychology, 15*:5 (1968), pp. 393–401.

(27) Tosi, D. J., R. D. Briggs, and R. M. Morley, "Study Habit Modification and its Effect on Academic Performance: A Behavioral Approach," *Journal of Educational Research, 64* (1971), pp. 347–50.

(28) Tosi, D. J., K. Upshaw, A. Lande, and M. Waldron, "Group Counseling with Non-Verbalizing Elementary Students: The Differential Effects of Premack and Social Reinforcement Techniques," *Journal of Counseling Psychology, 18*:3 (1971), pp. 437–40.

(29) Tosi, D. J., R. Vanderhill, R. Hanel, and W. Balinger, "The Differential Effects of Short-Term Social Reinforcement and Rational-Emotive Counseling on Discipline Problem Students," unpublished ms., 1971.

(30) Truax, C. C., H. Fine, J. Moravic, and W. Mills, "Effects of Therapist Persuasive Potency in Individual Psychotherapy," *Journal of Clinical Psychology, 24* (1968), pp. 259–76.

(31) Valins, S., "Emotionality and Autonomic Reactivity," *Journal of Experimental Research in Personality, 2* (1967), pp. 41–48.

(32) Velton, E., "A Laboratory Task for the Induction of Mood States," *Behavior Research and Therapy, 6* (1968), pp. 473–82.

(33) Walton, D. and M. D. Mather, "The Relevance of Generalization Technique to Treatment of Stammering and Phobic Symptoms," *Behavior Research and Therapy, 1*(1963), pp. 121–25.

9 Similarities and Differences

In the preceding chapters six major systems of verbal psychotherapy/counseling have been examined. What may appear to be differences in the detail of these examinations is but a reflection of the varying degrees of complexity and development of the theories themselves. Each theory is at a different stage of organization, and, of course, the more organized theories appear to be covered more comprehensively.

The theories were selected for examination on the basis of a count of references to them in the major journals most appropriate to counselors.* Many other theories might have been selected, but few theories other than the ones examined are even mentioned in the chosen journals. How many additional counseling theories there are would be difficult to estimate, and selection would depend upon the criteria applied by the investigator. Harper counts thirty-six (8). Some are not very well organized and seem to have no current following; some are also essentially group psychotherapies, none of which is considered here. During a general search for theoretical material, we found forty-three distinct, fairly well organized therapies in the literature. Each of these therapies seems to have at least a small following. These forty-three therapies all emphasize individual rather than group counseling.

There is no great significance to these forty-three therapies as far as this study is concerned. It was necessary to read over a wide range of psychotherapeutic theory in order to discuss in detail the

*See chapter 1 for details on choice of journals used.

six theories chosen for this text. Brief summaries of these and other theories are found in the appendix. We entertain no illusion that the summary statements will receive universal acceptance by the community of therapists.

In the summarization of these theories the name commonly given to the theory is stated, along with the principal writer associated with the therapy. The general approach of the theory is rated as objective or subjective. The subjective therapies focus primarily on man's inner reality. Objective therapies tend to be more instrumental and outer-reality centered. Related theories of personality are also listed to give the reader a more complete picture of the theory. The "central ideas" are based on interpretation rather than on some single statement from the major writer. The central-idea statements are admittedly brief but hopefully germane.

The forty-three systems listed should be considered as a minimum number of possible theories as each counseling therapist, in a sense, has something different to say about a theory. Even writers in the same theoretical camp can not agree. In addition, many of Harper's theorists are not included in the list because they did not seem appropriate or relevant for a background for school counseling. One look at these theories and the reader can appreciate Ungersma's comment: "The present situation in psychotherapy is not unlike that of the man who mounted his horse and rode off in all directions" (23, p. 55). In a sense each writer in the field of counseling is riding off on a horse in a different direction. Many of these riders may pass through the same canyon and hence gain some common identification as to direction, but the riders are still individual in their horsemanship.

Certainly the picture is one of diversity, a diversity that has led many a reviewer to despair.* In the hope of establishing some order, we tried to organize the selected theories along a standard outline and to suggest some meaningful comparisons.

The organization presented problems. A great deal of material on Roger's theory is available in his own writings, and the theory fits the selected outline rather well. But with the other theories there were more problems.

Williamson's writings are diverse and sketchy as far as theory is concerned. There is no single work or even series of works that

---

*The *1969 Annual Review of Psychology* did not publish a section on counseling/ psychotherapy because the reviewer could not get the material organized for publication.

gives enough material about his theory for the purposes of this book. His theory has to be constructed by bits and pieces from many sources. Williamson's own current summary of his theory is not complete in this respect (26).

With behavioral counseling the problem was different. Behavioral approaches receive much attention but are organized less than almost any of the theories. It is even difficult to discern just who the behaviorists are since they are all in the learning theory family. It also was difficult to choose the spokesman for the family. Other writers attempting to evaluate theory either talked in such generalities that any learning theorist would fit (6), or they chose an individual theorist and wrote about him (15; 5; 20). An attempt was made to read all the theorists identified in any writing as behaviorists and group together those theorists who held what seemed to be cohesive, common views. The behaviorist view was constructed from this common ground.

In a sense, the evaluation of the existentialists was similar in complexity to that of the behaviorists. The existentialist theory is either completely avoided in the writings of those who attempt to summarize theories (22), or one existentialist writer is chosen and the rest ignored (15). Sahakian includes an article by Frankl and three articles from May's book (20). The May work and the Frankl work are handled separately. Other writers base their work mainly on the May work (5). The key difficulty in studying the existential therapists is to group them on common theoretical grounds without diluting their individual ideas.

No phrase has seemed to catch on in the literature of guidance and counseling like *developmental guidance* or *developmental counseling.* The phrase has not caught on, however, in the literature of theorists or those who deal in the comparison of theories. None of the books which handle theoretical approaches mention the idea of developmental counseling. It is only recently (early 1970s) being mentioned in counseling as distinct and separate from the more global concept of developmental guidance. It is a theory which has to be pieced together from a number of different authors and is a relatively new, loosely organized conceptualization.

At the present time, the rational-emotive counseling theory is primarily based on work by a single author (Albert Ellis) with some additional writing contributions by Robert A. Harper. As a system of counseling, rational-emotive counseling has not achieved the detailed organization of some of the older counseling theories.

The unique organization and synthesis of these six theories of counseling should aid the reader in his understanding of counseling theory in general and these six theories in particular, with a concern for their respective possibilities in school counseling. A clear attempt has been made to present each theory along a common outline. An effort is also made to present the theoretical essentials of each theory devoid of excessive verbiage, illustrations, or case materials. By this strategy the reader can easily compare elements of an individual theory with like elements in another theory. Some of the theoretical writers have ancillary parts to their theories. Others attempt to illustrate their theory with interview transcripts. None of these elements is included in this book. The only elements chosen for inclusion are those that fulfill the rubrics of the theoretical outline. Readers having a particular interest in one or more of these theories may wish to consult the bibliography for more extensive and supplementary reading. Since each theory is forced into a common outline, some of the theoristic embellishments and case materials do not appear in this discussion. Many of the writers also have supplementary and complementary positions that do not deal directly with their theory of counseling but can sometimes be helpful in understanding the total impact of the theory.

Similarities and differences among these theories are examined in a number of areas. The first area is the background of the principal writers in each of the theories.

BIOGRAPHICAL COMPARISONS

Nearly all of the theorists concerned with these six systems represent the traditional White Anglo-Saxon background. Most of the writers were trained in this country. Of those trained in the United States, Rogers, Blocher, Ellis, Williamson, May, Moustakas, van Kaam, Krumboltz, Schaefer, and Martin were trained primarily as clinical psychologists. Peters, Farwell, Shertzer and Zaccaria were primarily prepared in counseling and guidance, more recently known as counselor education. The remaining U.S. trained psychologist is Skinner, who is primarily an experimentalist. Eysenck was trained in clinical psychology in the United Kingdom. Frankl, Binswanger, and Ellenberger were medically trained in Vienna, Switzerland, and the Union of South Africa respectively. Wolpe and Lazarus also received training in South Africa, the former in medicine and the latter in psychology.

The developmental writers have the common ground of work in public education at either the elementary or secondary level. Williamson's work has also been influenced by education but at the college student personnel level.

Most of the client-centered therapists were trained and worked in clinical psychology. The behaviorists, for the most part, are also practicing therapists. Skinner would be the exception.

The widest range of experience is found within the ranks of the existential therapists. Three are practicing psychiatrists; one, a psychoanalyst; and two, practicing clinical psychologists.

Since none of the therapists represented cultures very different from traditional Western culture, it is interesting to speculate how much more dissimilar the system would have been had an Eastern, or some other culture, been represented. One could also speculate as to the influence on the systems of the Greco-Judaeo-Christian tradition, which underlies much of Western culture.

Finally there seem to be some restrictions placed on the kinds of people treated by these theorists. The trait-factor counselors write primarily about college populations. Developmentalists seem primarily interested in adolescents. With the exceptions of Schaefer and Martin, the behaviorists prefer to deal with nonhospitalized patients, though Eysenck handles both hospitalized as well as nonhospitalized patients. Most of the existentialists and rational-emotive counselors see patients in clinics rather than residential settings. With the exception of Moustakas, who is primarily concerned with young children, the existentialists work with adults.

Essentially the emphasis of nearly all the theorists seems to be on normal individuals in some varying degree of psychological discomfort. The terms *normal* or *neurotic* accommodate the theoretical population better than the term *psychotic.*

THE NATURE OF MAN

Man's essential nature has been described by all of the theorists covered in this examination, perhaps less so in the rational-emotive approach. These descriptions vary in length, emphasis, and organization. Some "schools" emphasize man's nature considerably more than do others. The existentialists write much more to this interest than do the behaviorists. The developmental writers seem to give most of their views by implication rather than direct discussion. Although Blocher accepts Beck's views, he states none of his own (1). Williamson's text has a lengthy discussion about the nature of man, but his own views are not complex (25). Client-centered therapists have a positive view of man that is unique among the five theories. Rogers' writings reflect a Rousseauist view of man, which conceives him as being basically good (3). Rogers says also that man is rational and self-actualizing (17).

The other theorists all write of man as essentially neutral; that is, he has the equal potential for good or evil. They do have some supplementing views to go along with the essential position of neutrality. Williamson agrees with Rogers' conception of man's rationality but is not as inclined to accept self-actualization. The trait-factorist sees himself as a strong influence in self-actualization. The existentialists more or less agree with the self-actualization or, as they would say, freedom to become, but may question rationality, as they write of man in strongly subjective terms. The behaviorists, after accepting the neutrality of man's nature, concern themselves with man's behavior as being, rather than self-actualizing, a result of reinforcements acting upon him from his environment. The developmental writers accept the neutrality of man's nature, but the rest of the views concerning man are as diverse as the individual writers. Ellis refuses to deal with the dichotomy by considering the good or evil question as simply a premise without empirical basis.

There is a great deal of similarity within the "schools" of counseling/psychotherapy represented in this study. Whether this similarity stems from the Judaeo-Christian ethic fundamental to the writers or is a reflection of some fragment of truth which seems common to counselors is unclear.

Whether man is at birth essentially good (Rogers) or neutral, neither good nor bad (existentialists, trait-factorists, behaviorists or developmentalists), is not an easy question to answer. Whether man is essentially in control of his own life (Rogers, Ellis, and existentialists) or controlled by his life (Williamson and behaviorists) or somewhere in between (developmental view) is an equally difficult question. These two concerns about man's nature have always been the Gordian knot for both psychologists and philosophers. As essential as it is for man to hold such views about himself, since they reflect on his whole system of life, it must be accepted that resolution of these views may well be impossible. The simplest problem of life remains its most complex.

PERSONALITY THEORY

The theories of therapy examined vary considerably as to their dependence on or association with personality theory. Rogers places considerable emphasis on personality, while the existentialists and the developmental counselors give it no emphasis at all. Existentialists use their philosophic view of man in a way not unlike the way other theorists use personality theory. Developmental counselors do not write of personality theory but seem to emphasize an orderly developmental sequence. These sequences are nearly identical with the maturational developmental concepts found in nearly all personality theories and particularly those found in developmental psychology. Even though the developmentalists do not write of personality theory, they seem to base many of their ideas of counseling on maturational, developmental personality theory.

Roger's theory of personality is a well-organized theory. It is a synthesis of phenomenology as presented by Snygg and Combs, holism and organismic theory as developed by Goldstein, Maslow, and Angyal, and of Rogers' own self-theory (7, p. 478). Nearly all of Rogers' recent summaries of his theory illustrate the importance of this theory of personality.

Between Rogers' emphasis on personality and the developmentalists' and existentialists' nonemphasis are the positions of the behavioral, rational-emotive, and trait-factor counselors.

The behaviorists and rational-emotive counselors rely on personality theories that stress learning as a basis. Behaviorists stress the importance of learning theory, but which learning theory stressed depends upon the writer. Skinner's, Shoben's, Murray's, and Maslow's theories are mentioned for consideration as basic theories of personality. Careful reading of the behaviorist theorists uncovers even more theoretical possibilities. Of all the learning theories Mowrer's two-factor theory seems to fit most appropriately.

The trait-factor theorists have an emphasis very similar to the learning theorists. The most appropriate personality theory seems to be that of Eysenck and Cattell (7, ch. 10). To these ideas Williamson adds many of his own (25, pp. 204–5). The added ideas appear to be built upon the earlier offerings of Eysenck and Cattell.

The trait-factor counselors and the client-centered therapists have apparently formulated their theories of personality out of their counseling experiences. Their theories are modifications of existing personality theories. The behaviorists, on the other hand, appear to have started with theories of behavior and personality and developed therapy from these.

The existentialists, for the most part, seem to have absorbed philosophical existentialism congruently with therapy practice. As yet they and the developmentalists have no developed theory of personality. Landsman has criticized therapists for this theoretical neglect (9).

CONDITIONS OF COUNSELING

Not all of the counseling or therapeutic systems examined mention any conditions of therapy. The developmentalists, the rational-emotive counselors, and the existentialists avoid writing about any necessary conditions for counseling. However, it is inconceivable that counselors from any of these schools would impose no limits or conditions on the therapeutic exchange. In essence, the conditions of therapy are but assumptions stated in advance about the counselor, client, or the relationship. All theories have some assumptions, but only three of the theories covered in this examination seem to put emphasis on the conditions.

Client-centered therapists list six conditions which are "necessary and sufficient" if the process of therapy is to take place. These conditions deal with the counselor, client, and the relationship. Behavioral counselors stress three responsibilities for the counselee in the relationship. These responsibilities or conditions precede the counseling process, as is the case with the client-centered view.

Williamson's list of conditions is by far the most elaborate. He lists seventeen conditions, with the comment that there are probably many more. Williamson's conditions for the interview deal with the relationship between counselor and student, the purposes of counseling, and the counselor himself.

The conditions of therapy seem to be related to the theory itself. Much of the fiber of the theory is woven within those ideas that each of the writers identify as conditions. The number of conditions listed, however, seems to have no direct relationship to the complexity of the theory. Existentialism lists none; trait-factor lists seventeen. It would be dangerous to judge the adequacy of theory solely on the listing of conditions of therapy. These listings give only some indication of the comprehensiveness and order in the therapeutic system.

PROCESS OF THERAPY

The process of therapy is covered in relative detail by all of the theorists. Process is, however, a classification of events, feelings, thoughts, and assumptions that has different meanings among the various systems. The developmentalists, for instance, who have no conditions of therapy, list a process of "limits" which encompasses the same set of ideas as the behaviorists' three conditions of therapy. Therapists do not appear to be very consistent in their process-condition listings, probably because of the interdependence of the two elements in counseling.

Each of the theories has a number of processes which all deal with what the client is doing or experiencing. In client-centered therapy, there is no emphasis, as such, on the counselor or the relationship. The relationship is considered only as the background which allows the client to think or act in a particular way.

The trait-factor processes are, on the other hand, mostly directed toward the counselor. The implementive emphasis of the theory is seen in this focus. The counselor does this and that. There is little to indicate student strivings as in the client-centered viewpoint.

Behaviorists list eight processes which are strongly related to learning theory and reinforcement. Even though the list of processes is rather short, many elements are covered, including client changes, therapist direction and relationship elements.

Developmental counselors' eight elements also have to do with the counselor, the client, and the relationship. The eclectic or borrowing nature of the developmental writers is seen in their process list.

Existentialist writers vary somewhat in their emphasis on process. Although the content of the process as seen from the existentialist point of view is quite different from the other views, it does include the same category of elements; that is, relationship, client, and therapist variables.

Rational-emotive therapists write of a number of elements which could easily fit into the category of process, although they are not identified as such. The main emphasis, however, seems to be on two elements: the ABC process and homework.

Diagnosis is discussed, as a process, in five of the six theoretical positions. Rogers' position is one exception. For other theorists it has varying degrees of importance. The existentialists are seemingly split on the practice elements of diagnosis. Frankl and Binswanger stress it, as their treatments are relatively categorical. May and Moustakas, on the other hand, do not appear to use diagnosis at all as part of the counseling process. The behaviorists use the term only when it describes a client's functions. Diagnosis as a trait description is totally rejected.

For Williamson diagnosis is an extremely important element. As important as it is to his counseling process, however, it is very simply described as cooperative interpretation. Both the counselor and the student must put effort into diagnosis in Williamson's view. The developmentalists have five levels within their diagnostic system. This may sound like an uncommon complexity, but it must be remembered that most of the European existentialists have a diagnostic category for each classification of disorder. The developmentalists' classification has to do with the level of functioning of the individual. These levels range from "panic," no control at all, to "mastery," complete control. The rational-emotive counselor must diagnose to determine the extent and direction of the client's irrationality.

Diagnosis is important to the theoreticians who vary the counseling process according to the diagnostic category. It is unimportant for those therapists who use essentially the same process, with possibly different emphasis, on all clients.

TECHNIQUES OF COUNSELING

The issue of techniques in counseling has been an interesting one indeed. Existentialists and client-centered therapists have not stressed techniques as they seem to view them as manipulative. Within these views is the strong conviction that the client should express his own feelings and striving to become. If the counselor would apply techniques to him, how could the client become anything but what the counselor wanted him to become? But, once again, the pendulum seems to swing back toward a recognition of techniques within these two schools. Both C. H. Patterson, client-centered, and May, existentialist, have recently written about techniques.

Techniques seem either to have been highly manipulative or highly philosophical and nonmanipulative. These vary with the system. The techniques of the existentialists and the client-centered therapists in the main would be considered nonmanipulative. Behaviorists list eight techniques which would be considered by most as very manipulative or reinforcing.

The techniques also seem to vary as to their specificity. Client-centered techniques are very general, while the developmentalistic and the trait-factor writers are quite explicit.

The rational-emotive counselor uses teaching techniques to show the client the rules of straight thinking and logical living. Behaviorists, for example, place emphasis on learning principles; hence their techniques reflect this interest. Rogerians stress self-actualization; hence their techniques reflect this emphasis. The trait-factor counselors probably have as their most important technique the use of psychometric devices, a technique very important to one who is interested in the objective quantification of data and the nomothetic approach.

Technique is not an idle position of the counselor, but a way of life within the interview. It would be interesting to speculate upon a relationship where one person came to another for assistance, and the latter had no technique with which to work.

GOALS OF COUNSELING

There are a number of ways to look at goals, and each writer has his own preferences. Each of Rogers' goals of counseling states what the client would or should become. These goals closely follow the processes of therapy. A very similar approach is demonstrated by the existentialists. Although they have only seven goals listed, these goals also deal with potential or becoming behavior.

Behavioral goals have to do with more learning and manipulative matters. Alteration of behavior and learning solutions to problems are key elements in the goals as stated. Somewhat related to this approach is the method used by Williamson in stating his goals. The role of the counselor here is also somewhat instrumental. Counselors are to help students choose goals and gain self-understanding. Counselors are to be used by students in seeking the "good life."

All of the developmental goals are stated in terms of what developmental counseling could do for clients. Yet some of the goals resemble those of existential counseling, while others are more behavioral in tone.

There seem to be about three general opinions among these therapists as to who selects goals. The behaviorists and the rational-emotive therapists tend generally to select the goals of therapy or treatment for their patients. These therapists allow the patient some choice, to be sure, but the counselor determines which behavior patterns are disordered and which need to be modified.

Another common opinion seems to be that the client himself must take the responsibility for selecting goals. Client-centered and existential therapists seem to share this view. The subjective self-actualizing emphasis of these theories are consistent with such a type of goal selection.

The third way of looking at goal selection is one where there is a great deal of mutual participation in the selection of goals. Close to this view are the trait-factor theorists and the developmentalists. The trait-factor counselor would let the student and the counselor mutually decide on a goal, but from then on the counselor would take much of the responsibility. Much the same view is held by Blocher as goal selection is seen as a meeting of the counselor's philosophy and the client's self-perceptions. The rational-emotive approach is well organized in this direction.

The goals of counseling tend to be stated in high-level abstractions that, when traced to specifics, often produce confusion. How do we know if the student is seeking the good life? Or what is the good life? How do we know when a client is self-actualizing? The goals or ideals of man do appear, however, to be the ultimate abstractions. This is the way man has always looked at the ideal. Counseling theory should be no different in spite of the evaluative difficulties.

THEORY AND SYSTEM

Some philosophers and scientists seem to argue endlessly about the appropriateness of counseling or psychotherapeutic theory. Whether counseling deserves the word *theory* or *art* is a question as well as an admonition of many writers. One problem of classification has been that some writers are content to consider theory only in the sense of natural sciences. Others consider it as a philosophical examination (16). Chenault states: "With the exception of Pepinskys' contribution [1954], there is really no such thing as counseling theory" (2, p. 110). Nagel, on the other hand, has identified the theory difference between natural science and social science. He states that theory, as it relates to social science, is compositive or synthetic rather than analytic (14, p. 363). A theory is "any more or less formalized conceptualization of the relationship of variables" (11, p. 43).

According to this concept of theory, all of the writings covered within this examination could be classified as theory. The theories even fulfill the criteria for a system since a system is "an organization and interpretation of the data and theories of subject matter with emphasis upon a particular methodology and working assumptions" (11, p. 43).

The question of theory or system alone is not enough. It is necessary to consider the adequacy of the theories. Maddi has suggested six over-all criteria for evaluating the adequacy of theory (10, pp. 451–59). Many positions may fulfill the criteria for theory and still not be adequate. The ideas of theory and adequacy are related but separate.

The first criteria is that of importance. There could be little argument as to the importance of psychotherapeutic theory. The second point is that a theory should be operational. Operational simply means that the meaning of a concept is determined by the measurement operations associated with it. Here there has been some disparity among the systems. The client-centered counselors have painstakingly operationally defined and researched many of their concepts. The behaviorists with their learning background have done the same, even though from a different vantage point. Trait-factor theorists have had many of their assumptions tied to assumptions inherent in psychological measurement and therefore have been at least marginally operational. Neither the existentialists, who have not stressed operationism, nor the developmentalists and rational-emotive therapists whose theories are just beginning to grow, would fulfill the criteria for formal operational adequacy.

The third element of theoretical adequacy is precision. None of the theories has yet attained clear and precise use of concepts and terms. These counseling theories are filled with figurative, metaphorical, and ambiguous terms. The client-centered and the behavioral therapists are probably less guilty than the other theorists on this point. Both theoretical positions have made efforts to state their terms and operations clearly.

Related to these considerations is the idea that a theory should be empirically valid. Empirical validity has been, and may continue to be, the most difficult area of evaluation in counseling theory.

> So complex is the behavior of a living thing, so intertwined the reaction of subject and investigator that one wonders whether

the behavioral scientist can ever achieve the precision, the validity . . . or the replication . . . available to the physical sciences
(19).

The empirical test of any theory is the predictability of outcome. At
this point in the development of counseling theory empirical observations are probably more effective than empirical tests.

The last of Maddi's over-all criteria for judging the adequacy of
theory has to do with the usability and parsimony of theory. Counseling theories are very usable, particularly to the originator of the
theory. They have been useful in ordering and evaluating behavior
even if they are imprecise. As to parsimony, theories do not measure
up very well. Many counseling theories are uncommonly complex,
beyond evaluation. Over-simplication is the danger in the other direction. The only real judge as to whether a theory is oversimplified
or parsimonious is time and empirical validation.

As imprecise as counseling theory is, it still remains the only
logical device by which a counselor can investigate and test assumptions. Without some theory there would be no framework within
which to interpret findings. Counseling would become a set of *ad hoc*
responses and impulsive improvisations. Clearly these theories need
a great deal of research and refinement, but without them there is
no place to go.

OTHER COMPARISONS

There are many other ways in which one could
compare theories. These ways are grouped together in this section
because the comparisons are not so detailed. Some of the comparisons are quite subtle and inferential.

Theories could be judged on a realist, phenomenalist objective
continuum. In a phenomenalist counseling theory the assumption is
that valid knowledge of the world is impossible to agree on (client-
centered, existentialist). In a realist counseling theory the assumption is that valid knowledge of the world is possible (trait-factor,
rational-emotive, behaviorists). At this time in the organization of
developmental theory it is difficult to place the theory at either end
of this realist-phenomenalist scale. Developmentalists express statements which are sometimes realistic and sometimes phenomenalis-
tic. The phenomenalist counselor tends to help deepen the client's
unique perceptions, while the realist counselor generally helps his

clients to see how the world really is and how it appears to others (21).

Judging the theories as to internal consistency is another method for comparison (18). Existential, client-centered, and behavioral counseling theories are internally consistent. The Rogerians and existentialists use indeterministic goals and methods, while the behaviorists use deterministic goals and methods. Developmental and trait-factor counselors are internally inconsistent. The developmentalists have indeterministic goals and deterministic methods. The trait-factor counselors have deterministic methods and goals, but state them in indeterministic terms (18).

The theories considered can also be divided on the "Protestant Ethic" (individual concern) versus the "Social Ethic" (group concern) scale. Rational-emotive therapy does not clearly fit either of these categories. The existentialist, developmentalist, and client-centered views are reflections of the "Protestant Ethic," while trait-factor and behavioral counseling reflect the "Social Ethic."*

Theories also differ in their use of terminology. The object of counseling or therapy is called *client* (client-centered, rational-emotive), *student* (trait-factor), or *patient* (existential). Some of the behavioral counselors use the word *patient,* and some use *client.* Developmental counselors use the words *client* and *counselee.* With the exception of the existentialists and behaviorists, the person working with the client is called a *counselor.* Existentialists use the term *therapist* as do some of the behavioral counselors. Other behavioral counselors also use *counselor.*

The word *interview* is usually applied to the relationship between the principals of counseling (Rogers and developmental). At times trait-factor counselors use *seminar* to describe the interplay between counselor and student. The behaviorists and existentialists not using the term *interview* prefer *therapy session.*

These uses of terminology add possibly more than subtle differences to the theorists. A client is essentially an equal, while a patient is one who has come for help generally in the form of diagnosis and treatment. The use of *counselee* is semantically a normal progression of the process of counseling, but it is also seen as a kind of revolt against the clinic-oriented vocabulary of some counselors. Williamson's use of *student* is an obvious extension of his student-personnel-work orientation. The term *therapist* has a stronger deterministic

---

*See discussion of the Protestant Ethic and Social Ethic in Romines' work (18).

ring than *counselor. Counseling* may be most any kind of relationship, but *therapy* has the connotation of direct help and manipula-
tion.

CONCLUSION

Each of the theories has been forced into a com-
mon outline. Some of the theories resist the force, but all are finally
placed. The choice of the theories, although theoretically justified in
the early part of this work, is, in the final analysis, idiosyncratic. The
choice of outline is another element that reflects the individuality of
the investigators.

Any writer or writers would be a bit egocentric to undertake an
evaluation of someone else's work feeling he could add to the author's meaning. The urge here was to outline theoretical constructs
of the most written about theories in the field of counseling and
guidance, especially as found in school counselor education preparation programs. The words *behaviorist, developmentalist,* and others
are bandied about with great relish by writers in our field. Some of
these writers discuss theories which have yet to be very well formulated. Writers in the field have not undertaken organization of the
existentialist position, only the position of individual existentialists.
The developmental counseling or guidance movement is a movement without an organized theory. No one has organized the theory
from the various developmental writers. As old as the psychological
field of behaviorism is, there is no organization of the behavioral
counseling model. Individual learning theorists are occasionally
evaluated. Occasionally someone labels one of these learning theorists a behaviorist and writes a summary of his views. An effort was
made here to give form and organization to the developmental, behavioral, and existential views.

For the purposes of this evaluation it was even necessary to
reorganize the trait-factor theory. This theory, even though it has
been around for thirty years, is still difficult to organize. The elements of the theory appear in scattered form. Even when found, they
are difficult to identify because Williamson does not organize his
ideas systematically. Rogers' theory remains the best organized for
this research. It fits well into the outline. Ellis' approach appears to
be just that—an individualized approach of one therapist rather
than a counseling theory. His views are just beginning to generate
the necessary research and interest for validation.

Some readers may feel that too much was attempted in this review and comparison. Others may feel that the comparisons lack objectivity or even subjectivity. In the end, value judgments, hopefully thoughtful, dictated all evaluations. These value judgments are stated in chapter 1 as well as identified throughout this book where they were relevant to discussion. Some unevenness of discussion is due to the obvious unevenness of the theory presented.

It was with respect and admiration that an organization and evaluation such as this is even attempted. Writers of counseling theory and practice have shared their dedication, sensitivity, and clinical skill so as to help push back the darkness. These men have made contributions to society as well as to the smaller world of counseling. The fact that they have fallen short of the ideal theory does not mean they have failed. They are on their way. In the last analysis some combination of hard-headed empiricists and starry-eyed speculators will discover the ideal rubrics for theory, probably in a number of frameworks. Those theoretical offerings that have preceded us deserve our attention and respect, attention when we attempt to examine detail and respect for the theorists' organization and views of what is ultimately an extension of his personality. Tribal acceptance is as fruitless as complete denial. Dogma-eat-dogma is great sport as a spectacle but intellectually profitless. Probably what is needed, along with theory development in counseling, is the genuine implementation into practice. The discrepancies today between theoretical pronouncements and real involvement in counseling lead to the phoniness against which so many youth rebel (24). The talk, more sophisticatedly called *dialogue,* continues. And this is important. One needs only several illustrations to be reminded of the "talk." Mills discusses the implications that culture cyclically changing from affective predominance to cognitive predominance has for counseling and counseling techniques (13). What guidance and counseling is best for blacks is a major question of the seventies (27). Are the present counseling theories relevant? Sandra Dahl presents provocative questions related to the phoniness and realities of counseling theory and practice (4). She states: "The activist counselor realizes that most of the truly important messages are not yet to be found in our own professional literature . . ." (4, p. 697). They come from biologists, poets, and other disciplines of learning and media sources.

Is it not time that we—counselor educators, state supervisors, school counselors and other pupil services staff—be alert to, speak on, and act to meet the critical needs of children, youth, and even adults of this time and place?

References

(1) Blocher, Donald H., *Developmental Counseling* (New York: The Ronald Press Company, 1966).

(2) Chenault, Joann, "Counseling Theory: The Problem of Definition," *Personnel and Guidance Journal, 47* (October, 1968), pp. 110–14.

(3) Coulson, William, "Client-Centered Therapy and the Nature of Man," Ph.D. diss., University of Notre Dame, 1964.

(4) Dahl, Sandra, "Who Is Building the Bridges?" *Personnel and Guidance Journal, 49* (May, 1971), pp. 693–97.

(5) Ford, Donald H. and Hugh B. Urban, *Systems of Psychotherapy: A Comparative Study* (New York: John Wiley & Sons, Inc., 1963).

(6) Goodstein, Leonard D., "Behavioral Theoretical Views of Counseling," in B. Stefflre (ed.), *Theories of Counseling* (New York: McGraw-Hill Book Company, 1965), pp. 140–92.

(7) Hall, Calvin S. and Gardner Lindzey, *Theories of Personality* (New York: John Wiley & Sons, Inc., 1957).

(8) Harper, Robert A., *Psychoanalysis and Psychotherapy: 36 Systems* (Englewood Cliffs, N.J.: Prentice-Hall, Inc., Spectrum Books, 1959).

(9) Landsman, Ted, "Personality Theory and Counseling," in D. S. Arbuckle (ed.), *Counseling and Psychotherapy: An Overview* (New York: McGraw-Hill Book Company, 1967), pp. 164–73.

(10) Maddi, Salvatore R., *Personality Theories: A Comparative Analysis* (Homewood, Ill.: Dorsey Press, 1968).

(11) Marx, Melvin H., "The General Nature of Theory Construction," in M. H. Marx (ed.), *Theories in Contemporary Psychology* (New York: The Macmillan Company, 1963), pp. 4–46.

(12) May, Rollo, Ernest Angel, and Henri Ellenberger (eds.), *Existence: A New Dimension in Psychiatry and Psychology* (New York: Basic Books, Inc., Publishers, 1958).

(13) Mills, David H., "Counseling in the Culture Cycle: Feeling or Reason," *Personnel and Guidance Journal, 49* (March, 1971), pp. 515–22.

(14) Nagel, Ernest, *Logic without Metaphysics* (Glencoe, Ill.: The Free Press, 1956).

(15) Patterson, C. H., *Theories of Counseling and Psychotherapy* (New York: Harper & Row, Publishers, 1966).

(16) Peterson, James Allan, *Counseling and Values: A Philosophical Examination* (Scranton: International Textbook Company, 1970).

(17) Rogers, Carl R., "Nondirective Counseling: Client-Centered Therapy," in W. S. Sahakian (ed.), *Psychotherapy and Counseling* (Chicago: Rand McNally & Company, 1969), pp. 169–209.

(18) Romines, Willie Hester, "An Examination of Four Positions in Counseling in terms of Selected Educational and Sociological Variables," Ph.D. diss., University of Alabama, 1967.

(19) Rubin-Rabson, Grace, "Behavioral Science versus Intelligence," *Wall Street Journal, 49* (July 1, 1969), p. 12.

(20) Sahakian, William S. (ed.), *Psychotherapy and Counseling: Studies in Technique* (Chicago: Rand McNally & Company, 1969).

(21) Schell, Edith and Edward Daubner, "Epistemology and School Counseling," *Personnel and Guidance Journal, 47* (February, 1969), pp. 506–13.

(22) Stefflre, Buford (ed.), *Theories of Counseling* (New York: McGraw-Hill Book Company, 1965).

(23) Ungersma, Aaron J., *The Search for Meaning* (Philadelphia: Westminster Press, 1961).

(24) _____ *Escape from Phoniness* (Philadelphia: Westminster Press, 1969).

(25) Williamson, E. G., *Vocational Counseling: Some Historical, Philosophical, and Theoretical Perspectives* (New York: McGraw-Hill Book Company, 1965).

(26) _____ "Vocational Counseling: Trait-Factor Theory," in B. Stefflre (ed.), *Theories of Counseling* (New York: McGraw-Hill Book Company, 1965), pp. 193–214.

(27) "What Guidance for Blacks?" *Personnel and Guidance Journal, 48* (May, 1970), entire issue.

Bibliography

Allers, Rudolf, *Existentialism and Psychiatry* (Springfield, Ill.: Charles C. Thomas, Publisher, 1961).

Arbuckle, Dugald S. (ed.), *Counseling and Psychotherapy: An Overview* (New York: McGraw-Hill Book Company, Inc., 1967).

Ard, Ben N. Jr. (ed.), *Counseling and Psychotherapy* (Palo Alto, Calif.: Science and Behavior Books, Inc., 1966).

Beck, Carlton E., *Philosophical Guidelines for Counseling,* 2nd ed. (Duquesne, Iowa: William C. Brown Co., 1971).

Biggs, Donald A., John D. Roth, and Stanley R. Strong, "Self-Made Academic Predictions and Academic Performance," *Measurement and Evaluation in Guidance, 3* (Summer, 1970), pp. 81–85.

Bingham, Walter Van Dyke and Bruce Victor Moore, *How to Interview,* 3rd ed. (New York: Harper & Brothers, Publishers, 1941).

Breisach, Ernst, *Introduction to Modern Existentialism* (New York: Grove Press, Inc., 1962).

Bry, Adelaide, *Inside Psychotherapy* (New York: Basic Books, Inc., Publishers, 1972).

Delaney, Daniel J. and Sheldon Eisenberg, *The Counseling Process* (Chicago: Rand McNally & Company, 1972).

DiLoreto, Adolph O., *Comparative Psychotherapy: An Experimental Analysis* (Chicago: Aldine Publishing Company, 1971).

Dugan, Willis E. (ed.), *Counseling Points of View* (Minneapolis: University of Minnesota Press, 1959).

Dunlop, Richard S. (ed.), *Professional Problems in School Counseling Practice* (Scranton: International Textbook Company, 1968).

Eysenck, Hans J., *The Structure of Human Personality* (London: Methuen & Co. Ltd., 1953).

―――― "Learning Theory and Behavior Therapy," in H. J. Eysenck (ed.), *Behaviour Therapy and the Neuroses* (London: Pergamon Press, Inc., 1960).

Hart, J. T. and T. M. Tomlinson, *New Directions in Client-Centered Therapy* (Boston: Houghton Mifflin Company, 1970).

Hersher, Leonard, *Four Psychotherapies* (New York: Appleton-Century-Crofts, 1970).

Hutt, Max L., Robert L. Isaacson, and Milton L. Blum, *Psychology: The Science of Interpersonal Behavior* (New York: Harper & Row, Publishers, 1966).

Kell, Bill L. and Josephine Morse Burow, *Developmental Counseling and Therapy* (Boston: Houghton Mifflin Company, 1970).

Kelly, George A., *A Theory of Personality: The Psychology of Personal Constructs* (New York: W. W. Norton & Company, Inc., 1963).

Krech, David and George S. Klein, *Theoretical Models and Personality Theory* (New York: Greenwood Press, Inc., 1968).

Lee, Edward N. and Maurice Mandelbaum, *Phenomenology and Existentialism* (Baltimore: Johns Hopkins Press, 1967).

May, Rollo, "The Origins and Significance of the Existential Movement in Psychology," in R. May, E. Angel, and H. Ellenberger (eds)., *Existence: A New Dimension in Psychiatry* (New York: Basic Books, Inc., Publishers, 1958) pp. 3–36.

Niehaus, Stanley W., "The Counselor Menagerie, or What to Avoid in Counselors," *The School Counselor, 13* (November, 1965), pp. 242–46.

Omvig, Clayton P., "Effects of Guidance on the Results of Standardized Achievement Testing," *Measurement and Evaluation in Guidance, 4* (April, 1971) pp. 47–52.

Parker, Clyde A. (ed.), *Counseling Theories and Counselor Education* (Boston: Houghton Mifflin Company, 1968).

Patterson, C. H., *Counseling and Psychotherapy: Theory and Practice* (New York: Harper & Brothers, Publishers, 1951).

_____ *An Introduction to Counseling in the School* (New York: Harper & Row, Publishers, 1971).

Pepinsky, Harold B. and Pauline Nichols Pepinsky, *Counseling Theory and Practice* (New York: The Ronald Press Company, 1954).

Pervin, L. A. "Existentialism, Psychology, and Psychotherapy," *American Psychologist, 15* (1960), pp. 305–9.

Peters, Herman J. and Michael J. Bathory, *School Counseling* (Itasca, Ill.: F. E. Peacock, Publishers, Inc., 1968).

Phillips, E. Lakin and Daniel N. Wiener, *Short-term Psychotherapy and Structured Behavior Change* (New York: McGraw-Hill Book Company, 1966).

Rogers, Carl R., "Some Observations on the Organization of Personality," *American Psychologist, 2* (September, 1947), pp. 358–68.

Sahakian, William S. (ed.), *History of Psychology* (Itasca, Ill.: F. E. Peacock, Publishers, Inc., 1968).

Singer, Erwin, *Key Concepts in Psychotherapy* (New York: Random House, Inc., 1965).

Stefflre, Buford and W. Harold Grant, *Theories of Counseling*, 2nd ed. (New York: McGraw-Hill Book Company, 1972).

Stollak, Gary E., Bernard G. Guerney, Jr., and Meyer Rothbery (eds.), *Psychotherapy Research* (Chicago: Rand McNally & Company, 1966).

Tolbert, E. L., *Introduction to Counseling,* 2nd ed. (New York: McGraw-Hill Book Company, 1972).

Tyler, Leona A., *The Work of the Counselor,* 3rd ed. (New York: Appleton-Century-Crofts, 1969).

APPENDIX

Individual Counseling Theories

Name of Theory	Principal Writer	General Approach	Related Theory of Personality	Central Idea
Behavioral counseling	John Krumboltz	Objec.	Learning	Importance of selective reinforcement in the reeducation of clients; highly implementative role of the counselor.
Behavior therapy	Hans Eysenck	Objec.	Learning	Importance of reinforcements in the determination of behavior.
Character analysis	Karen Horney	Subjec.	Modified psychoanalytic	Underlying principle of human behavior the need for security.
Client-centered	Carl Rogers	Subjec.	Rogerian	Human behavior determined by man's perception of himself and his environment.
Communications theory counseling	Frank Robinson	Objec.	None	Importance of counselor remarks and techniques on client responses.
Conditional reflex therapy	Andrew Salter	Objec.	Learning	Stress on reconditioning; stress on excitation as basis of life, and overcoming of inhibition.
Constructive alternativism psychotherapy	George Kelley	Objec.	Learning	Man has many workable alternative ways in which to construct his world.

Name of Theory	Principal Writer	General Approach	Related Theory of Personality	Central Idea
Direct psychoanalysis	John Rosen	Objec.	Psychoanalytic	Deviation on psychoanalysis; stresses role playing and even physical contact with patients.
Developmental counseling	Donald Blocher	Objec./ Subjec.	Maturational developmental	The maximizing of human freedom and effectiveness in all men.
Ego-analysis	Heinz Hartmann David Rapaport Anna Freud	Objec.	Freudian	Emphasis on human instrumental behaviors (ego-functions).
Ego and milieu therapy	John Cummings Elaine Cummings	Objec.	Psychoanalytic	Emphasis upon how a person meets situations (ego) in his environment (milieu).
Existential analysis	Henri F. Ellenberger	Subjec.	None	Man strives to find meaning in life.
Existential analysis and psychotherapy	Ludwig Binswanger	Subjec.	None	Man must realize the fullness of his humanity.
Existential psychotherapy	Rollo May	Subjec.	None	Man must recognize and experience his own existence.
Experiential or nonrational psychotherapy	Carl Whitaker Thomas Malone	Subjec.	None	Therapeutic emphasis upon feeling, rather than intellect (non-rational), and upon the feeling experience (experiential) between therapist and patient.
Gestalt psychotherapy	Frederick Perls Ralph Hefferline Paul Goodman	Subjec.	Lewin's Gestalt Theory	Emphasis on the organism-as-a-whole; organism-environment unity must be maintained.

Therapy	Proponents		Orientation	Description
Hypnotherapy	Lewis Wolberg	Objec.	None	Understanding of anxiety with the use of hypnosis.
Individual psychology	Alfred Adler	Objec.	Adlerian	Importance of patient's life style; stress on life goals and social interest.
Interference theory: Assertion-structured therapy	E. Lakin Philips	Objec.	Learning	Man selects behavior consciously. Behavior patterns of man can be understood by his choices (assertions).
Interpersonal therapy	Harry Stack Sullivan	Subjec.	Modified psychoanalytic	Importance of interpersonal relations and significant others in one's life.
Implosive therapy	Robert Hogan	Objec.	Learning	Therapist stresses maximum anxiety experiences so patient can become used to handling them.
Learning theory psychotherapy	John Dollard Neal Miller	Objec.	Learning	Man must be taught new conditions of life if his higher mental processes cannot solve emotional and environmental problems.
Logotherapy	Victor Frankl	Subjec.	None	Man suffers from loss of ultimate meaning to his existence that would make life worthwhile.
Milieu therapy	Maxwell Jones Robert Rapoport	Objec.	None	Emphasis on psychotherapeutic value of all members of a hospital staff.
Minimum change theory	Leona Tyler	Objec.	None	A relatively minor change in the psychological direction in a client's life will produce considerable change over a long time.
Personality counseling (Also called directive counseling or eclectic counseling)	Frederick Thorne	Objec.	None	Emphasis on a comprehensive integration of scientific data to form an eclectic system for handling client problems.

157

Name of Theory	Principal Writer	General Approach	Related Theory of Personality	Central Idea
Psychoanalysis	Sigmund Freud	Objec.	Psychoanalytic	Importance of unconscious and early childhood as determinant of behavior.
Psychoanalytic therapy	Franz Alexander	Objec.	Psychoanalytic	A more flexible application of Freudian techniques.
Psychobiologic theory	Adolf Meyer	Objec.	None	Stresses unity of mind and body whether they are functioning adequately (well) or inadequately (sick).
Psychological counseling	Edward Bordin	Objec.	Psychoanalytic	The responsibility of the counselor to contribute positively to the client's emotions and motivations by removing the underlying obstacles to psychological growth.
Rational-emotive psychotherapy	Albert Ellis	Objec.	Learning	Emotion is controllable by rational thinking processes.
Reality therapy	William Glasser	Objec.	None	Clients who are in difficulty are unwilling to take the responsibility for their behavior.
Reciprocal inhibition psychotherapy	Joseph Wolpe	Objec.	Learning	Elimination of an unwanted response, such as anxiety, by pairing the anxiety-producing stimulus with another stimulus not having anxiety-producing tendencies, to systematically desensitize patient.
Reinforcement counseling	Harold Pepinsky Pauline Pepinsky	Objec.	Learning	Counselor as both practitioner and scientist; continuous use of observation, inference, and assessment of client behavior.

Approach	Person	Orientation	Theory base	Description
Semantic therapy	Wendell Johnson	Objec.	None	Emphasizes patient's use and understanding of language as key to eliminating conflicts.
Social learning theory counseling	Julian Rotter	Objec.	Learning	Emphasis on importance of social learning and a system of constructs that will provide maximum prediction and control of behavior.
Social-psychological analysis	Erich Fromm	Subjec.	Psychoanalytic	Man's needs are based on his existence as a social animal.
Systems approaches	T. A. Ryan	Objec.	None	Counseling based upon a consideration of a series of sub-parts or topics organized into a unified flow of events.
Therapeutic psychology	Lawrence Brammer Everett Shostrom	Objec./ Subjec.	Psychoanalytic/ developments	Importance of using ideas that are useful no matter where they may be found.
Transactional analysis	Eric Berne	Objec.	Psychoanalytic	Importance of understanding an individual's behavior in groups.
Transactional approach	Roy Grinkr	Objec.	Psychoanalytic	Stresses the transaction between therapist and patient in which neither person exists as a separate individual but each acts in relation to the other.
Trait-factor counseling	E. G. Williamson	Objec.	Learning	The importance of psychometrics in helping a student understand himself and his environment.
Will therapy	Otto Rank	Subjec.	Initially psychoanalytic	Will as an expression of positive, unifying, and creative aspects of an individual's striving toward independence.

Name Index

Adler, Alfred, 66
Albert, Gerald, 5, *9*
Allen, Thomas W., 20, *22, 42*
Allers, Rudolf, *152*
Allport, G. W., 21, *22*
Anderson, S. C., 126, *130*
Andrews, W. R., 91, 92, *93*
Angel, Ernest, 65, 66, 67, *76, 150, 153*
Angyal, A., 31
Arbuckle, Dugald S., 2, *9,* 21, *22,* 45, 56, 57, *59,* 63, 72, *75,* 79, *93,* 101, *111, 150, 152*
Ard, Ben N., Jr., 48, 50, *61, 113, 152*
Armor, David, 41, *42*
Aubrey, Roger F., 2, *9*
Ayllon, T., 126, *130*
Azrin, N. H., 126, *130*

Balinger, W., 127, *132*
Bandura, Albert, 80, 84, 85, *93*
Barnes, H. E., 63, 64, *78*
Bates, Marilyn, 66–67, *75*
Bathory, Michael J., *153*
Beck, Carlton E., 51, *60,* 74, *152*
Benson, Ronald L., 56, 58, *60*
Berelson, Bernard, 21, *22*
Berenson, Bernard G., 85, 87, 88, *94,* 97, 101, *112,* 126, *130*
Berger, Louis, 80, *93*
Bernstein, A., 126, *131*
Bertocci, Peter A., 20–21, *22*

Biggs, Donald A., 109, 110, *111, 152*
Bijou, Sidney W., 80, 82–83, 87, *93*
Bingham, Walter Van Dyke, *152*
Binswanger, Ludwig, 67, 70, *76*
Bischof, Ledford J., 25, 31, *42*
Blocher, Donald H., 5, *9, 22,* 46–58, *60,* 138, *150*
Blum, Milton L., *152*
Bordin, Edward S., 4, *10, 105,* 107, *111*
Boring, Edward G., 16, *22*
Bower, Gordon H., 86, *94*
Boy, Angelo V., *42*
Brammer, Lawrence M., 4, *10,* 45, 46, 49, 51, *60*
Breisach, Ernst, *152*
Briggs, R. D., 126, *132*
Brodbeck, May, 13, *22*
Bry, Adelaide, *152*
Burkhead, D. E., 125, 126, *130*
Burow, Josephine M., 47, *60, 152*

Caldwell, Charles E., 47, *60*
Carkhoff, Robert R., 21, *22,* 85, 87, 88, *94,* 97, 101, *112*
Carlson, W. A., 125, 126, *130*
Cartwright, Rosalind Dymond, 19, *22*
Chaplin, J. P., 15, 16–17, *22*
Chenault, Joann, 144, *150*
Chmeron, William B., *22*
Cohen, Morris R., 14, *22*
Colby, Kenneth M., 3, *10*

Italic numbers refer to references.

Subject Index